FINANCIAL ACCOUNTING

Palgrave Business Briefings

The *Business Briefings series* consists of short and authoritative introductory text-books in core business topics. Written by leading academics, they take a no-nonsense, practical approach and provide students with a clear and succinct overview of the subject.

These textbooks put the needs of students first, presenting the topics in a meaning-ful way that will help students to gain an understanding of the subject area. Covering the basics and providing springboards to further study, these books are ideal as acces-sible introductions or as revision guides.

Other books in the Business Briefings series:

Research Methods, by Peter Stokes & Tony Wall

Marketing, by Jonathan Groucutt & Cheryl Hopkins

Organizational Behaviour, by Mike Maughan

Human Resource Management, by Michael Nieto

Quantitative Methods, by Les Oakshott

Management Accounting, by Jill Collis

The Business Briefings Series
Series Standing Order ISBN 978–0–230–36385–4

You can receive future titles in this series as they are published by placing a standing order. Please contact your bookseller or, in the case of difficulty, write to us at the address below with your name and address, the title of the series and the ISBN quoted above.

Customer Services Department, Macmillan Distribution Ltd, Houndmills, Basingstoke, Hampshire, RG21 6XS, UK

FINANCIAL ACCOUNTING

JILL COLLIS

 palgrave

First published 2016 by
PALGRAVE

Palgrave in the UK is an imprint of Macmillan Publishers Limited, registered in England, company number 785998, of 4 Crinan Street, London, N1 9XW.

Palgrave Macmillan in the US is a division of St Martin's Press LLC, 175 Fifth Avenue, New York, NY 10010.

Palgrave is a global imprint of the above companies and is represented throughout the world.

Palgrave® and Macmillan® are registered trademarks in the United States, the United Kingdom, Europe and other countries.

ISBN 978–1–137–33588–3

This book is printed on paper suitable for recycling and made from fully managed and sustained forest sources. Logging, pulping and manufacturing processes are expected to conform to the environmental regulations of the country of origin.

A catalogue record for this book is available from the British Library.

A catalog record for this book is available from the Library of Congress.

Printed in China

CONTENTS

List of Figures		vi
List of Tables		vii
Preface		viii
Acknowledgements		x
1	INTRODUCTION TO FINANCIAL ACCOUNTING	1
2	THE ACCOUNTING SYSTEM	15
3	FINANCIAL REPORTING FRAMEWORKS	39
4	STATEMENT OF COMPREHENSIVE INCOME	61
5	STATEMENT OF FINANCIAL POSITION	84
6	STATEMENT OF CASH FLOWS	108
7	CONSOLIDATED FINANCIAL STATEMENTS	130
8	FINANCIAL STATEMENT ANALYSIS	152
References		179
Answers to Revision Questions		181
Index		231

LIST OF FIGURES

1.1	UK private sector enterprises by legal status	8
1.2	Types of business entity	12
2.1	Source documents for selling goods	16
2.2	Source documents for purchasing goods	16
2.3	Overview of the accounting process	17
3.1	Fundamental accounting principles	43
3.2	Primary users of general purpose financial reports	51
3.3	Qualitative characteristics of useful financial information	55
5.1	Classifying assets, equity and liabilities	86
8.1	Main types of ratio	153
8.2	Ted Baker PLC Report and Accounts 2014 (extract)	154–157
8.3	Ten-year trend in Ted Baker's operating profit margin	172

LIST OF TABLES

1.1 Worldwide membership of UK and Irish accountancy bodies 2
1.2 Main features of public and private companies 13
3.1 Financial reporting size thresholds 47
3.2 Set of financial statements 56
4.1 Examples of fair value 73
6.1 Main adjustments to operating income and expenses under the indirect method 120
8.1 Ten-year analysis of Ted Baker's operating profit margin 172

PREFACE TO FINANCIAL ACCOUNTING

With tuition fees at a high level, many students find the purchase of a traditional text-book is something that they have to compromise on, and either rely on the lecturer's handouts or borrow books from the library or friends. Unfortunately, this approach is rarely successful as it can only provide a partial and superficial understanding of the subject. This is particularly true of accounting, which many students find difficult.

The book is part of Palgrave's 'Business Briefings' series. It is designed to be succinct, but cover the basics of the subject. This means it is likely to be much more affordable. Students will still need to consult other texts to widen their knowledge of the subject, but this book offers a good introduction and can easily be used for revision purposes.

Most accounting courses taught in universities and colleges follow a syllabus that reflects the professional exams taken by accountants. This book covers the main topics associated with financial accounting in a logical sequence. It starts by explaining the accountancy profession and the nature and purpose of accounting, and setting the business context. It then moves on to explain the double-entry bookkeeping system and how the trial balance provides data for preparing the annual financial statements. This is followed by an explanation of the fundamental accounting principles, the main elements of the regulatory framework and the conceptual framework that underpins the development of International Financial Reporting Standards. Sequential chapters take the reader through the preparation of financial statements for a small company. Attention then switches to the preparation of consolidated financial statements for a group entity. The focus on large companies continues in the final chapter, which explains the techniques used to analyse published financial statements.

Each chapter has the same structure:

Objectives
Introduction
Main content
Key points
Revision questions

The main content of each chapter explains the basics of the topic, and case studies are used as examples or to show how the techniques are applied. The case studies are chosen to reflect business reality and some are real business cases.

The key points section is a useful summary of the chapter and will be invaluable as part of a revision strategy. The revision questions are based on the material covered in the chapter and should allow the reader to gauge his or her understanding of the concepts and techniques covered. Solutions and indicative model answers to these questions can be found at the end of the book as well as on the companion website: www.palgrave.com/companion/Collis-Financial-Accounting.

ACKNOWLEDGEMENTS

The author is grateful to Roger Hussey and Andrew Holt for permission to adapt some of their material for use in this book.

The author and publishers would like to thank Ted Baker PLC for permission to use the data from their 2014 financial report.

1

INTRODUCTION TO FINANCIAL ACCOUNTING

1.1 OBJECTIVES

This chapter provides an introduction to accounting in a business context, and financial accounting in particular. After studying this chapter, you should be able to:

- Identify the main professional accountancy bodies.
- Explain the need for a code of ethics for professional accountants.
- Explain the nature and purpose of accounting.
- Distinguish between financial accounting and management accounting.
- Compare different types of business entity.

1.2 THE ACCOUNTANCY PROFESSION

A professional accountant in the UK or the Republic of Ireland must pass a number of rigorous examinations set by one of the recognised accountancy bodies and pay an annual subscription to become a member of that body. The examinations cover a wide range of topics such as business and finance, financial and management accounting, financial reporting, auditing, taxation, law, business strategy and financial management. Table 1.1 shows the worldwide membership of the chartered accountancy bodies, plus one other body that offers a recognised audit qualification, at 31 December 2014.

Once qualified, accountants can set up in practice on their own or with partners, or seek employment in an existing accountancy practice. Others may choose to work as accountants in industry and commerce, or in the public or voluntary sectors. Some accountants qualify with a view to working in the family business, and those with entrepreneurial ideas may choose to start a new enterprise.

Large businesses are likely to have sufficient resources to employ a number of accounting and finance specialists, whereas medium-sized entities may employ one

Table 1.1 Worldwide membership of UK and Irish accountancy bodies

	Number	%
Association of Chartered Certified Accountants (ACCA)	174,227	36
Institute of Chartered Accountants in England and Wales (ICAEW)	144,167	30
Chartered Institute of Management Accountants (CIMA)	99,942	20
Chartered Accountants Ireland (CAI)	23,778	5
Institute of Chartered Accountants in Scotland (ICAS)	20,401	4
Chartered Institute of Public Finance and Accountancy (CIPFA)	13,327	3
Association of International Accountants (AIA)	9,250	2
Total	485,092	100

Source: FRC, 2015, p. 11

accountant who is responsible for financial and management accounting functions, supported by other staff, such as a credit controller and bookkeeper. Very small entities often find it more cost effective to use an external accountant.

Professional accountants have a duty to serve the public interest because they are involved in the preparation and auditing of published financial information. Accountants and auditors are guided in their work by a code of ethics. *Ethics* are moral principles that underpin what is considered right and wrong in society, and how people should behave (Waite, 2012).

> **Activity**
> How ethical are you? Imagine you came out of a restaurant and found that the waiter had not charged you for your dessert. Would you go back and tell him?

You have to ask yourself whether you would be happy to tell everyone (not just your friends, but your family and your teachers or boss) and how you would defend your actions if you were challenged. An ethical person would go back and tell the waiter or the manager, so the correct answer is 'Yes'. The important thing to realise is that ethics are not always about what other people might do, but about honesty and personal integrity.

The need for high values and consistent, ethical behaviour across the accountancy profession led to the development of an international code of ethics by the International Ethics Standards Board of Accountants (IESBA). The *Code of Ethics for Professional Accountants* (the IESBA Code) is published by the *International Federation of Accountants (IFAC)*, which is an association of professional bodies of accountants throughout the world. IFAC was founded in 1977 and in 2014 had 172 members and associates in 129 countries and jurisdictions, representing approximately 2.5 million accountants (including those in Table 1.1).

The IESBA Code requires a professional accountant to comply with five fundamental principles (IESBA, 2013, para 100.5):

(a) Integrity – to be straightforward and honest in all professional and business relationships.

(b) Objectivity – to not allow bias, conflict of interest or undue influence of others to override professional judgments.

(c) Professional Competence and Due Care – to maintain professional knowledge and skill at the level required to ensure that a client or employer receives competent professional services based on current developments in practice, legislation and techniques and act diligently and in accordance with applicable technical and professional standards.

(d) Confidentiality – to respect the confidentiality of information acquired as a result of professional and business relationships, and, therefore, not disclose any such information to third parties without proper and specific authority, unless there is a legal or professional right or duty to disclose, nor use the information for the personal advantage of the professional accountant or third parties.

(e) Professional Behavior – to comply with relevant laws and regulations and to avoid any action that discredits the profession.

Activity

Jane Goodfellow is an accountant at Vinyl Products Ltd. She recently noticed that the price of one of the materials used in the production process had gone up significantly, and this coincided with a change of supplier. When she tried asking the purchasing manager, Simon Buckfast, about it, he more or less told her to mind her own business, adding, "I've known the managing director of this new supplier for years and, in any case, it's my job to decide which suppliers we use!" Around this time, Jane also noticed that Simon had started driving an expensive new car to work. She suspects that the two events are connected, which might indicate fraud. Should she (a) turn a blind eye, (b) challenge Simon further, or (c) discuss the matter with another senior manager?

The facts are that the cost of materials has risen as a result of changing the supplier and Simon is responsible for the decision. Jane has an ethical dilemma because she is concerned about Simon's dismissive response, weak justification for the change in supplier, and luxurious new car. She suspects fraud and wonders what the best action would be. To ensure that she behaves with integrity, objectivity and professional competence, she should take action (b) followed by (c) if necessary.

1.3   NATURE AND PURPOSE OF ACCOUNTING

In its broadest form, accounting is a service provided to those who need financial information. In everyday language, *accounting* for something means giving an explanation or report on something. The following definition is taken from the *Oxford Dictionary of Accounting*.

Definition

Accounting is the process of identifying, measuring, recording and communicating economic transactions.

Source: Law, 2010, p. 6

This book is concerned with the role of accounting in the private sector rather than public or voluntary contexts, so *economic transactions* refer to the money-making activities of the business that are directed at creating wealth for the owner(s). We will now examine each stage in the accounting process:

- Identifying economic transactions is fairly straightforward in most cases. Examples include selling goods and services to customers, paying employees, purchasing inventories (goods for resale) and buying equipment (for use in the business) from suppliers. It is also important to distinguish between the economic transactions of the business and the personal economic transactions of the owner(s) and manager(s). Thus, the first stage in the accounting process leads to the classification of the economic transactions of the business into categories, such as purchase, sales revenue and salaries.

- Measuring economic transactions in monetary terms is convenient. It also makes it easier to aggregate, summarise and compare transactions.

- Recording economic transactions is essential. Traditionally transactions were recorded in handwritten books of accounts known as ledgers, but today most businesses record transactions in a computerised accounting system. Small businesses may use spreadsheets or a simple accounting software package, but larger businesses with a wider range and volume of transactions use sophisticated software that may form part of an enterprise resource planning system.

- Communicating economic transactions is achieved by generating a variety of financial statements from the records in the accounting system. These are presented in a format that summarises a particular financial aspect of the business.

Activity

A business buys 5 litres of paint and 20 metres of timber, and employs a carpenter for two days to build shelves in an office. Paint costs £4 per litre, timber costs £2.50 per metre and the carpenter charges £50 per day. What is the total cost of the shelves?

The cost can be calculated in a number of stages. You need to multiply the cost of paint per litre by the amount used. You also need to multiply the cost of timber per metre by the amount used. Finally, you need to calculate the cost of employing the carpenter by multiplying his daily rate by the number of days. The order in which you work out the figures does not matter, as long as you arrive at three figures which, when added together, make up the total cost of the job:

	£
Cost of paint (£4 × 5 litres)	20
Cost of timber (£2.50 × 20 metres)	50
Cost of labour (£50 × 2 days)	100
Total cost of the shelves	170

In more complex examples it is not so easy to identify and measure the economic events in monetary terms. We will be looking at some of these problems in subsequent chapters.

The *purpose of accounting* in the private sector is to provide financial information that helps the business achieve its objectives. This might be to maximise profits or to make sufficient profit to maintain the lifestyle desired by the owner(s).

1.4   OVERVIEW OF FINANCIAL ACCOUNTING

Accounting can be divided into two main branches: financial accounting and management accounting. The purpose of *financial accounting* is to provide financial information to meet the needs of external users (those not involved in managing the business). On the other hand, the purpose of *management accounting* is to provide managers with financial and other quantitative information to help them carry out their responsibilities for planning, controlling and decision making. The emphasis is on providing information to internal users that will help the business entity achieve its financial objectives. Unlike financial accounting, management accounting is not governed by regulations.

Definition

Financial accounting is the branch of accounting concerned with classifying, measuring and recording the economic transactions of an entity in accordance with established principles, legal requirements and accounting standards. It is primarily concerned with communicating a true and fair view of the financial performance and financial position of an entity to external parties at the end of the accounting period.

Source: Collis, Holt and Hussey, 2012, p. 15

The term *true and fair view* implies that the financial statements produced at the end of an accounting period (usually one year) are a faithful representation of the entity's economic activities. The financial statements of limited liability entities are drawn up within a regulatory framework and are prepared using a number of accounting concepts which have been established as general principles. Generally, an entity's financial statements are considered to give a true and fair view if they comply with the regulatory framework and accounting principles. We will discuss this in the next chapter.

Financial accounting can be divided into the following main activities:

- *Bookkeeping* focuses on the recording of business transactions. Most small businesses use spreadsheets or standard accounting software, while large businesses are more likely to need tailor-made software.
- *Accounts preparation* involves the compilation of financial statements for external users, such as shareholders, tax authorities, lenders or major suppliers and customers.
- *Auditing* involves a thorough examination of the entity's financial systems and records, tangible assets, management and employees, suppliers, customers and other business contacts. Auditors conduct compliance tests to assess the effectiveness of the systems of financial control and substantive tests to assess the completeness, ownership, existence, valuation and disclosure of the information in the accounting records and financial statements.

- *Corporate recovery* covers the provision of insolvency services and advice to companies in financial difficulty.
- *Advisory services* such as advice on taxation, raising finance, investment, pension planning, treasury management, IT and human resource management, or advice on running a business.

Although accounting can be divided into financial and management accounting, you should not be misled into thinking that there is no relationship between these two activities as they both draw on the same data. However, there are some important differences, which relate to the level of detail and timing of the information produced. Financial accounting operates on the basis of an annual reporting cycle, and the preparation of the financial statements of limited liability entities is highly regulated to ensure that external users receive high quality, reliable information. However, the annual report and accounts is not published until some months after the end of the financial year. By contrast, management accounting is not regulated at all, which means the information can be provided to internal users in the form they want it and as often as they want it. In both large and small businesses, detailed management accounting information for each activity in each part of the business is produced on a weekly, monthly or quarterly basis. If the periodic management accounts for the different parts of a business were aggregated, the totals would be very similar to the figures in the financial accounts, although there would be some differences. For example, the financial accounts would contain information on finance costs (such as interest paid on loans) and taxation, whereas the management accounts are likely to contain more estimated figures.

1.5   TYPES OF BUSINESS ENTITY

In the UK the legal form of businesses in the *private sector* can be classified into three main types:

- Sole proprietorships.
- Partnerships.
- Companies and other incorporated entities.

At the start of 2014, the number of private sector enterprises in the UK reached a record level of 5.2 million. Figure 1.1 shows how they were dispersed among the three main categories.

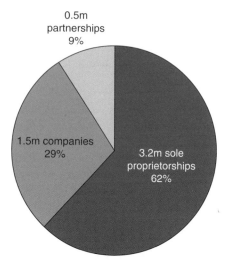

Figure 1.1 UK private sector enterprises by legal status
Source: BIS, 2014a, Table 3

The size of private sector enterprises ranges from very small businesses, such as sole proprietorships and one person companies with no employees, to large international companies with thousands of owners and employees. Of the total of 5.2 million businesses in the UK, 99.9% were small (fewer than 50 employees) or medium-sized (fewer than 250 employees) (BIS, 2014b, p. 1). In addition to providing a living for their owners, these small and medium-sized entities (SMEs) contributed to the economy by providing 60% of employment and 47% of turnover in the private sector.

The majority of smaller entities are owner-managed and family-owned (SBS, 2004; Collis, 2008). In larger businesses, it is more likely that ownership and control will become separated, and the owners will appoint managers to run the business on their behalf. Businesses also differ in terms of their legal status and in the groups of people who are likely to be interested in financial information about them.

To a large extent, the range of users of the financial information depends on the size of the business. For example, financial information relating to a small shop is likely to be used only by the owner-manager and the tax authorities, whereas financial information relating to a large international company will be of interest not only to managers within the business but also to investors, lenders, suppliers, customers and other external parties, such as competitors. Each user group needs financial information for a different purpose. A manager working in a division of a large company is likely to require detailed information in order to run the department, a bank lending officer contemplating lending £1 million to a business is likely to need information for assessing the lending risk and a supplier will need information for assessing the risk of supplying goods and/or services on credit to the business.

Accounting provides important financial information that helps businesses achieve their economic objectives. Some business owners want to increase their wealth by maximising profit while others simply want to make sufficient profit to maintain a certain lifestyle.

Sole proprietorships

The majority of businesses are *sole proprietorships*. A sole proprietorship is an unincorporated entity owned by one person who is in business with a view to making a profit. The business may be providing a service (for example, a window cleaner, hairdresser or business consultant), trading goods (for example a newsagent, florist or grocer) or making goods (for example, a cabinet maker, potter or dress designer). Alternatively, it may have activities in the primary sector (agriculture, forestry or fishing). The owner may run the business alone or employ staff.

The owner of a sole proprietorship has *unlimited liability*, which means that he or she is personally liable for any debts the business may incur. This liability extends beyond any original investment and could mean the loss of personal assets. There are no legal formalities to set up this type of business, but an entrepreneur wanting to start a sole proprietorship may experience difficulty in obtaining finance, as the capital is restricted to what he or she has available to invest, supplemented by what he or she can borrow. The owner must keep accounting records, but there is no obligation to disclose financial information to the public.

Partnerships

There are two types of *partnership*: unincorporated, ordinary partnerships and limited liability partnerships (LLPs). An *unincorporated partnership* is an entity in which two or more people join together in business with a view to making a profit. Unincorporated partnerships are a popular form of business for professional firms such as accountants, doctors, dentists and solicitors. The partners may run the business alone or employ staff.

The owners of an unincorporated partnership (the partners) have joint and several liability, which means they have unlimited liability for each other's acts in terms of any debts the business may incur. This liability extends beyond any original investment and could mean the loss of personal assets. The capital is restricted to what the partners have to invest, supplemented by what they can borrow. The *Business Names Act 1985* requires the names of the partners to be shown on business stationery, but they need not be used in the business name. The partners must keep accounting records, but there is no obligation to disclose financial information to the public.

The relationship between partners should be formalised in a partnership agreement. In the absence of a partnership agreement, or if the agreement does not cover a point in dispute, the *Partnership Act 1890* provides the following rules:

- Partners share equally in the profits or losses of the partnership.
- Partners are not entitled to receive salaries.
- Partners are not entitled to interest on their capital.
- Partners may receive interest at 5% per annum on any advances over and above their agreed capital.
- A new partner may not be introduced unless all the existing partners consent.
- A retiring partner is entitled to receive interest at 5% per annum on his or her share of the partnership assets retained in the partnership after his or her retirement.
- On dissolution of the partnership, the assets of the firm must be used first to repay outside creditors, second to repay partners' advances, and third to repay partners' capital. Any residue on dissolution should be distributed to the partners in the profit-sharing ratio (equally unless specified otherwise in the partnership agreement).

You may think that the partners do not need an agreement, because the Partnership Act 1890 sets out the relationship in case of dispute. However, relying on the Act means the rules of a standard agreement would be applied, which may not be appropriate to the circumstances.

Activity

Indicate which of these characteristics apply to the following types of business:

	Sole proprietorship	Partnership
(a) The entity is an unincorporated business	❏	❏
(b) There is no maximum number of owners	❏	❏
(c) There are no formalities involved when starting the business	❏	❏
(d) There should be a contract of agreement	❏	❏
(e) Accounting records must be kept	❏	❏

What sole proprietorships and unincorporated partnerships have in common is their unincorporated status, which means their owners have unlimited liability for any debts or losses incurred by the business. Of course, there is only one owner of a sole proprietorship, who is solely responsible, whereas the responsibility is shared in a partnership. A partnership can also raise more capital than a sole proprietorship because there it has at least two owners (there is no maximum number of partners). For the same reason, a greater range of skills is likely to be available in a partnership. There are no formalities involved in setting up a sole proprietorship, but the relationship between partners should be formalised in a partnership agreement. All businesses, regardless of legal status, must keep accounting records.

A *limited liability partnership (LLP)* is a partnership that through the process of incorporation acquires a legal status that is separate from that of its owners. An important advantage of an LLP is that each partner's liability for the debts and losses incurred by the business is limited to the amount of his or her investment in the business. There are two main exceptions to this limited liability:

- If a partner of an LLP is personally at fault, he or she may have unlimited liability if he or she accepted a personal duty of care or a personal contractual obligation.
- If an LLP becomes insolvent, the partners can be required to repay any property withdrawn from the LLP (including profits and interest) in the two years prior to insolvency. This applies where the partner could not reasonably have concluded that insolvency was likely.

LLPs are allowed to organise themselves internally in the same way as an unincorporated partnership, but the regulations that apply to them are similar to the requirements for companies. If one of the partners dies, his or her shares can be transferred to someone else and the business continues. On the other hand, when a partner in an unincorporated partnership dies, the partnership ceases. If the remaining partners want the business to continue, they need to form a new partnership, with or without additional partners.

Limited companies

The majority of limited liability entities are *limited companies*. A limited company is a business that through the process of incorporation acquires a legal status that is separate from that of its owners. The most common form of incorporation in the UK is through registration under the Companies Act 2006 (CA2006). The capital invested in the business is raised by selling shares to investors (hence the term *shareholder*), who are known as members. The capital invested in any type of business can be supplemented by loans and other forms of finance, such as trade credit from suppliers. Trade credit does not provide additional cash, but allows money already in the business to be used for other purposes until it is needed to pay creditors.

CA2006 defines a company as a limited company if the liability of its members is limited by its constitution. The company may be limited by shares or by guarantee. It is limited by shares if the members' liability is limited to the amount (if any) unpaid on the shares held by them. It is limited by guarantee if the members' liability is limited to such amount as they undertake to contribute to the assets of the company in the event of it being wound up.

> **Definition**
> Limited liability refers to the extent to which members of a limited company or LLP are liable for payment of the debts of the business.

Limited companies can be divided into *private companies* and *public companies*. More than 99% are private companies. A private company is any company that is not a public company. A public company is a company limited by shares or limited by guarantee and having share capital. Most companies are start as private limited companies. If a company grows sufficiently large, its owners may decide to convert it into a public company under the re-registration procedure in CA2006. This allows the company to obtain a listing on a stock exchange and raise large amounts of capital. There are around 2,600 companies listed on the London Stock Exchange. Listed companies are important because they make a substantial contribution to the economy. Table 1.2 (opposite) compares the main characteristics of public and private companies in the UK.

Figure 1.2 summarises the different types of business entity we have described.

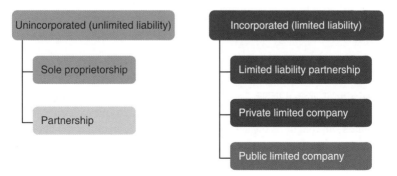

Figure 1.2 Types of business entity

Table 1.2 Main features of public and private companies

Public company	Private company
Must state in its memorandum of association that it is a public company	Defined as a company that is not a public company
Name must end with 'Public Limited Company' or 'PLC'	Name must end with 'Limited' or 'Ltd' or the Welsh equivalent
Can offer shares for sale on a stock exchange	Shares can be only be offered for sale privately
Must have at least one natural person not under 16 years of age as a director	Does not apply
Must have a company secretary (person or corporate) and hold an annual general meeting with members to pass resolutions	Does not apply
Must keep accounting records and publish financial statements complying with the Companies Act and accounting standards	Must keep accounting records and publish financial statements complying with the Companies Act and accounting standards
Must publish an annual report and accounts within 6 months of accounting year end	Must publish an annual report and accounts within 9 months of accounting year end
Extensive financial disclosure	Extent of financial disclosure depends on size and public interest

1.6   KEY POINTS

A professional accountant in the UK must pass a number of rigorous examinations set by one of the recognised accountancy bodies and pay an annual subscription to become a member of that body. Accounting can be divided into two main branches. Financial accounting focuses on providing financial information to be communicated to external users. Management accounting focuses on providing financial information to internal users. It is used by managers for planning, controlling and decision making to help the business achieve its financial objectives.

There are a number of different legal forms of business in the UK. An unincorporated enterprise can be a sole proprietorship or a partnership; an incorporated business can take the form of a limited liability partnership or a limited liability company. A limited liability company can be registered as a private company or a public company. The legal form of the business has financial implications in terms of ability to raise capital, disclosure of financial information and the owners' responsibility for the debts incurred by the business.

REVISION QUESTIONS

1. Describe how a student can become a qualified professional accountant and explain the need for a code of ethics for professional accountants.
2. Describe the key elements of the definition of accounting.
3. Compare and contrast the two main branches of accounting.
4. Explain the advantages and disadvantages of a setting up a one person business as a private limited company rather than a sole proprietorship.
5. Discuss the main differences between a public limited company and a private limited company in the UK, paying particular attention to the financial implications.

2
THE ACCOUNTING SYSTEM

2.1 OBJECTIVES

In order to generate financial information, a business needs to establish an accounting system in which to keep the accounting records. Some small enterprises keep a simple cash-based accounting system, but many businesses record transactions using a system known as *double-entry bookkeeping*. When you have studied this chapter, you should be able to:
- Explain the accounting equation.
- Describe and apply the principles of double-entry bookkeeping.
- Balance the ledger accounts.
- Prepare a trial balance.
- Discuss the limitations of a trial balance.

2.2 MAIN SOURCES OF DATA

All businesses are required to keep accounting records of the economic transactions and events. The nature of the accounting system depends on the type of business and the size of the organization. Typical procedures include raising *source documents* that record the details of the transactions. In many businesses, goods are purchased on credit and a number of external and internal documents are produced. Figures 2.1 and 2.2 summarize typical internal and external documents produced in connection with the selling of goods and the purchase of inventory (goods the business intends to sell).

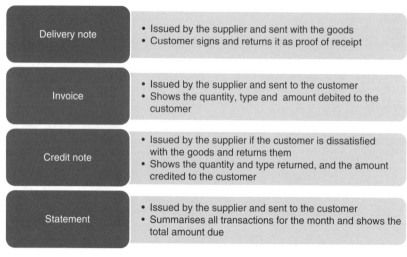

Figure 2.1 Source documents for selling goods

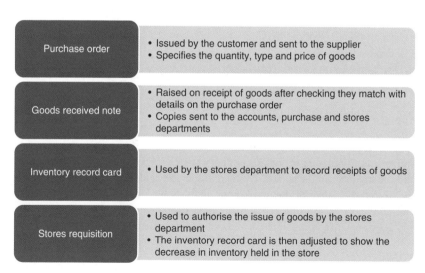

Figure 2.2 Source documents for purchasing goods

The business must also record labour costs so that the payroll office can calculate the wages and salaries paid to employees. Today the information is likely to be recorded in a computerised information system. In the service industry, *time sheets* may be used to record how much time has been spent on each job so that clients can be charged for the time spent on their work. Other important sources of information in the accounting system include cash receipts and payments, bank records and other documents.

Figure 2.3 provides an overview of the main stages in the accounting process. This chapter focuses on the first three stages.

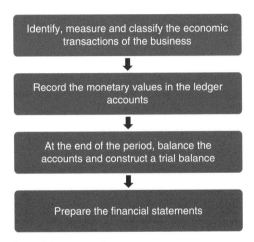

Figure 2.3 Overview of the accounting process

2.3 DOUBLE-ENTRY BOOKKEEPING

A double-entry bookkeeping system is based on the principle that every financial transaction involves the simultaneous receiving and giving of value. Therefore, every transaction needs to be recorded at least twice in the accounting system. This reflects the dual nature of economic transactions and ensures that an arithmetical check is made on the accuracy of the records. It is widely used because it is the most efficient and effective method for recording financial transactions in a way that allows financial statements to be prepared easily. The financial statements summarise the transactions that have taken place during any particular period of time. Most small businesses use Microsoft® Excel spreadsheets or accounting software such as SAGE. Large organisations carry out thousands of transactions every day and need sophisticated, tailor-made computerised accounting systems.

Definition

Double-entry bookkeeping is a method of recording the transactions of a business in a set of accounts, such that every transaction has a dual aspect and therefore needs to be recorded in at least two accounts.

Source: Law, 2010, p. 158

In order to understand double-entry bookkeeping, you need to remember that the business is a separate entity from its owners when it carries out transactions. Therefore, it can have dealings with the owners. All businesses need *assets*. These are what the business owns, such as premises, machinery, vehicles, equipment, inventory and cash. *Liabilities* are what the business owes to others apart from the owners, such as money owed to lenders and suppliers. What remains once the liabilities are subtracted from the assets is known as *equity*. Equity represents the owners' interest in the business and can be divided into the capital invested in the business by the owners and retained earnings (profits left in the business to help it grow).

Definitions

An asset is a resource controlled by the entity as a result of past events and from which future economic benefits are expected to flow to the entity.

A liability is a present obligation of the entity resulting from past events, the settlement of which is expected to result in an outflow from the entity of resources embodying economic benefits.

Equity is the residual interest in the assets of the entity after deducting all its liabilities.

Source: IASB, 2010a, para 4.4

The *accounting equation* illustrates the relationship between the assets, liabilities and equity. It lies at the heart of double-entry bookkeeping and reflects the dual nature of business transactions. The equation balances because it states that the assets are always equal to the claims against them (the equity and other liabilities).

Assets = Equity + Liabilities

> **Activity**
> A business has capital of £20,000 and assets of £20,000. It then borrows £10,000
> from the bank to finance the purchase of some new office equipment. How does
> this affect the accounting equation?

In this case the business has assets of £20,000 which will increase by £10,000 (the
new equipment), making total assets of £30,000. At the same time it will increase
its liabilities by £10,000 (the bank loan) whilst the equity, representing the capital
of £20,000, remains unchanged. The accounting equation still balances as shown
below.

Assets	=	Equity	+	Liabilities
£		£		£
20,000		20,000		10,000
10,000		____		____
30,000		20,000		10,000

If the business uses a manual system, the bookkeeper records the business transactions in the *ledgers*, which are books of accounts. Accounts for each different
type of transaction are kept on separate pages in the ledger. The bookkeeper
records every transaction as a *debit* entry in an account that receives the value
of the transaction and as a *credit* entry in an account that gives the value of
the transaction. The following illustration shows the layout. Debit entries are
shown on the left-hand side of the account and credit entries on the right.
On each side there is a column for the date, details of the transaction and the
amount involved. Because of their layout, ledger accounts are often referred to as
T accounts.

Name of the account

		£			£
Date	Details of debit entries	Amount	Date	Details of credit entries	Amount

2.4   RECORDING TRANSACTIONS

Recording assets and liabilities

The rules for recording transactions concerning assets and liabilities are:

- To show an increase in an asset account, debit the account.
- To show a decrease in an asset account, credit the account.
- To show an increase in a capital or liability account, credit the account.
- To show a decrease in a capital or liability account, debit the account.

Example

On 1 January this year, Nick Mulch started a business called Mulch Garden Design Ltd using £5,000 of his savings. His girlfriend, Louise, has given the business a loan of £2,000. All the money is kept in the bank. To record these transactions, we need to open three accounts: a *capital account* for the money invested by the owner; a *loan account* for the loan; and a *bank account* to show the bank transactions. There are two transactions to record: the amount invested by Nick and the loan given by Louise. Each transaction will require a debit entry to be made to one account and a corresponding credit entry of the same amount in another account.

Capital account

			£			£
				1 January	Bank	5,000

Loan account

			£			£
				1 January	Bank	2,000

Bank account

		£		£
1 January	Capital	5,000		
1 January	Loan	2,000		

As you can see, the investment of £5,000 by the owner has been shown as a credit in the capital account. Because the assets of the business have increased by this amount, the corresponding debit entry is in the bank account. When Louise gave the £2,000 loan to the business, its liabilities increased, so the loan account was credited with this amount. The corresponding debit entry is in the bank account, since the loan means an increase in the assets of the business.

We will now look at transactions made on 2 January. Using the business cheque book, Nick pays £3,000 for the premises, £1,000 for machinery and £500 for office equipment. The bank account is already open, but we need to open three new asset accounts to record these transactions.

Bank account

		£			£
1 January	Capital	5,000	2 January	Premises	3,000
1 January	Loan	2,000	2 January	Machinery	1,000
			2 January	Equipment	500

Premises account

		£		£
2 January	Bank	3,000		

Machinery account

		£		£
2 January	Bank	1,000		

Office equipment account

		£		£
2 January	Bank	500		

These records reflect the transactions that have taken place. For example, the bank account is an asset account. When the business received the investment of £5,000 from Nick and the loan of £2,000 from Louise, these amounts were debited to the bank account to show the increase in assets represented by the amount of money held at the bank. When the business paid for items such as the machinery, the bank account was credited. If you take the total of all the debit entries in the bank account and deduct the total of all the credit entries, the resulting figure is £2,500, which is the amount of money the business now has left at the bank.

> **Activity**
> Mulch Garden Design Ltd repays £1,500 of the loan to Louise on 3 January and on the same day returns £250 worth of faulty equipment to the supplier and receives a refund. Nick pays the refund into the bank. Enter these transactions in the ledger accounts.

The updated accounts look like this:

Bank account

		£			£
1 January	Capital	5,000	2 January	Premises	3,000
1 January	Loan	2,000	2 January	Machinery	1,000
3 January	Equipment	250	2 January	Equipment	500
			3 January	Loan	1,500

Loan account

		£			£
3 January	Bank	1,500	1 January	Bank	2,000

Office equipment account

		£			£
2 January	Bank	500	3 January	Bank	250

Recording revenue and expenses

Revenue (or *turnover*) is the income the business receives from its operating activities. In addition to revenue from sales to customers, the business may receive income from investment activities, such as bank interest, dividends on investments or rent received from letting part of the business premises. *Expenses* include the operating costs and any costs incurred in financing the business. You need to learn the formal definitions for these terms.

> **Definitions**
>
> Income is increases in economic benefits during the accounting period in the form of inflows or enhancements of assets or decreases of liabilities that result in increases in equity, other than those relating to contributions from equity participants.
>
> Expenses are decreases in economic benefits during the accounting period in the form of outflows or depletions of assets or incurrences of liabilities that result in decreases in equity, other than those relating to distributions to equity participants.
>
> Source: IASB (2010a, para 4.25)

The rules for recording transactions involving revenue and expenses are:

- To show an increase in an expense account, debit the account.
- To show a decrease in an expense account, credit the account.
- To show an increase in a revenue account, credit the account.
- To show a decrease in a revenue account, debit the account.

Example

On 4 January Mulch Garden Design Ltd spends £200 on advertising in the form of printed leaflets, and £20 on posting them to potential customers. Prior to this, the business had not incurred any expenses, so the monetary value in the advertising account and the postage account was nil. As you can see, these two expenses have decreased cash held in the bank.

Bank account

		£			£
1 January	Capital	5,000	2 January	Premises	3,000
1 January	Loan	2,000	2 January	Machinery	1,000
3 January	Equipment	250	2 January	Equipment	500
			3 January	Loan	1,500
			4 January	Advertising	200
			4 January	Postage	20

Advertising account

		£		£
4 January	Bank	200		

Postage account

		£		£
4 January	Bank	20		

Activity

On 5 January Mulch Garden Design Ltd pays £50 for having the premises cleaned. On 6 January the business lets its display gardens for a wedding reception and receives £350 in rent. Make the necessary entries in the appropriate revenue and expense accounts.

The cleaning expenses should be a straightforward pair of entries. The receipt of rent needs to be credited to a new revenue account called rent received, with a corresponding debit entry to the bank account showing an increase in cash assets of £350. The updated accounts look like this:

Bank account

		£			£
1 January	Capital	5,000	2 January	Premises	3,000
1 January	Loan	2,000	2 January	Machinery	1,000
3 January	Equipment	250	2 January	Equipment	500
6 January	Rent received	350	3 January	Loan	1,500
			4 January	Advertising	200
			4 January	Postage	20
			5 January	Cleaning	50

Cleaning account

		£		£
5 January	Bank	50		

Rent received account

	£			£
		6 January	Bank	350

Recording purchases, sales and inventory

A trading business needs goods to sell. *Purchases* of goods to sell are recorded in a purchases account as a debit entry. When the goods are sold, a sales account is opened. If the goods are sold for cash, the sale is shown as a credit in the sales account and a debit in the bank account to reflect the increase in cash assets held at the bank.

Example

Kate Burton opens a boutique called Kool Kate Ltd on 1 July by investing £10,000 in the business. On the same day the business buys equipment costing £1,000, purchases of inventory costing £4,000 and pays £500 in advertising expenses. On 2 July Kate makes sales amounting to £2,800 and buys a second-hand car for business use for £4,000. On 3 July she makes sales totalling of £3,500 and purchases further inventory for £2,000. The entries in the accounts are shown below.

Capital account

	£			£
		1 July	Bank	10,000

Bank account

		£			£
1 July	Capital	10,000	1 July	Equipment	1,000
2 July	Sales	2,800	1 July	Purchases	4,000
3 July	Sales	3,500	1 July	Advertising	500
			2 July	Vehicles	4,000
			3 July	Purchases	2,000

Equipment account

		£		£
1 July	Bank	1,000		

Advertising account

		£		£
1 July	Bank	500		

Purchases account

		£		£
1 July	Bank	4,000		
3 July	Bank	2,000		

Sales account

		£			£
			2 July	Bank	2,800
			3 July	Bank	3,500

Vehicles account

		£		£
2 July	Bank	4,000		

In this example we have referred to the goods that the business is buying and selling as *inventory*. However, we will not use an inventory account until the end of the accounting period, as we will explain in a moment. Instead, the purchases and the sales of goods have been recorded in separate accounts: the *purchases account* and the *sales account*. Accountants use the term *purchases* to refer only to the purchase of goods for resale in a trading business or the purchase of materials used to produce goods for sale in a manufacturing business. Do not confuse this with the acquisition of other assets, such as vehicles and equipment, which are not intended for resale but will stay in the business in the long term to help generate revenue.

Sometimes a business purchases goods, but returns some of them to the supplier because they are faulty, and sometimes a customer who has bought goods from a business returns them because they are faulty. The first transaction requires a *returns outward account* (also known as a *purchases returns account*) to be opened. The second transaction requires a *returns inward account* (also known as a *sales returns account*) to be opened.

Example

On 1 July Kool Kate Ltd purchases goods from a supplier, but a £200 dress was subsequently found to be faulty. It was returned to the supplier on 12 July and a refund of £200 was received the same day. These transactions are recorded as follows:

Bank account

		£			£
1 July	Capital	10,000	1 July	Equipment	1,000
2 July	Sales	2,800	1 July	Purchases	4,000
3 July	Sales	3,500	1 July	Advertising	500
12 July	Returns outward	200	2 July	Vehicles	4,000
			3 July	Purchases	2,000

Returns outward account

	£			£
		12 July	Bank	200

The bank account has been debited to show the increase in cash assets due to the cash refund by the supplier, but rather than crediting the purchases account to record the goods which were returned, a returns outward account has been opened and this provides an accurate record of what has happened. This information will be used when the statement of comprehensive income is drawn up later.

> ### Activity
> The same principles are applied if one of the customers returns goods. Show how the transactions would be recorded in the ledger accounts if a customer returns £500 worth of goods to Kool Kate Ltd on 14 July and is given a refund the same day.

The transactions would be recorded as follows:

Bank account

		£			£
1 July	Capital	10,000	1 July	Equipment	1,000
2 July	Sales	2,800	1 July	Purchases	4,000
3 July	Sales	3,500	1 July	Advertising	500
12 July	Returns outward	200	2 July	Vehicles	4,000
			3 July	Purchases	2,000
			14 July	Returns inward	500

Returns inward account

		£		£
14 July	Bank	500		

Credit transactions

All the transactions in the examples so far have been for cash, but many transactions are *credit transactions* where the receipt or payment of cash does not take place until a later date. This requires accounts to be opened for *trade receivables* to record the amounts owed to the business by customers, and accounts to be opened for *trade payables* to record the amounts the business owes to suppliers. Trade receivables are classified as assets of the business and trade payables are classified as liabilities. Therefore, we need to apply the rules for making entries in asset and liability accounts.

Example

Suppose the clothes sold for £2,800 to a customer called Pippa Merton by Kool Kate Ltd on 2 July were not cash sales but credit sales. The entry in the sales account will still be a credit, but instead of debiting the bank account to show an increase in cash assets, we need to open an account for Pippa Merton and debit that account to show an increase in the trade receivables asset. The entries in the accounts are as follows:

Sales account

		£			£
			2 July	Pippa Merton	2,800

Pippa Merton account (trade receivables)

		£			£
2 July	Sales	2,800			

Pippa Merton is a trade receivable account and we have followed the rules for an asset account. Before 2 July, Pippa owed the business nothing, but after the sales transaction on that date, she owed Kool Kate Ltd £2,800. The increase in trade receivables is shown by debiting the Pippa Merton account which was opened to record what this customer owes.

> **Activity**
> On 20 July Pippa Merton pays £750 of the money she owed to Kool Kate Ltd. Show how this transaction will be recorded in the accounts.

The accounts will be amended as follows:

Bank account

		£			£
1 July	Capital	10,000	1 July	Equipment	1,000
3 July	Sales	3,500	1 July	Purchases	4,000
12 July	Returns outward	200	1 July	Advertising	500
20 July	Pippa Merton	750	2 July	Vehicles	4,000
			3 July	Purchases	2,000
			14 July	Returns inward	500

Pippa Merton account (trade receivables)

		£			£
2 July	Sales	2,800	20 July	Bank	750

As you can see, cash assets have increased by £750 and the asset of trade receivables has decreased by the same amount. Note that we have deleted the entry in the bank account on 2 July for sales of £2,800 because Pippa Merton did not pay cash but took the goods on credit. Therefore, the debit entry is to the Pippa Merton account and the sales account remains unchanged.

Next we consider a case where the business has purchased goods or services on credit. The business has acquired a liability and we need to apply rules for increasing and decreasing liability accounts. On 26 July Kool Kate Ltd purchases goods for £1,500 on credit from a supplier, Patel & Co. On 28 July Kool Kate Ltd pays the amount in full. The transactions are recorded as follows:

Purchases account

		£		£
1 July	Bank	4,000		
3 July	Bank	2,000		
26 July	Patel & Co	1,500		

Patel & Co account (trade payables)

		£			£
28 July	Bank	1,500	26 July	Purchases	1,500

Bank account

		£			£
1 July	Capital	10,000	1 July	Equipment	1,000
3 July	Sales	3,500	1 July	Purchases	4,000
12 July	Returns outward	200	1 July	Advertising expenses	500
20 July	Pippa Merton	750	2 July	Vehicles	4,000
			3 July	Purchases	2,000
			14 July	Returns inward	500
			28 July	Patel & Co	1,500

These examples illustrate the principles of double-entry bookkeeping, which we will now summarise:

- A transaction that represents an increase in purchases, expenses or assets is recorded as a debit entry on the left-hand side of the ledger account.
- A transaction that represents an increase in revenue, liabilities or sales is recorded as a credit entry on the right-hand side of the ledger account.

You may find the following *pearls* of wisdom passed on by students across the decades help you remember these rules. The mnemonic is set out as a T account and reminds you that an increase in **P**urchases, **E**xpenses or **A**ssets is a debit entry shown on the left-hand, whilst an increase in **R**evenue, **L**iabilities or **S**ales is a credit entry shown on the right-hand side.

2.5   PREPARING A TRIAL BALANCE

Balancing the accounts

At the end of the accounting period the ledger accounts are balanced and the balances are used to construct a trial balance, which lists the debit balances in one column and the credit balances in the other. The rules for balancing the ledger accounts are:

1. If the total amounts on each side of the account are equal, there is no outstanding balance and they are double underlined to close the account. The trade payables account for Patel & Co account is an example of this.

Patel & Co account

		£			£
28 July	Bank	1,500	26 July	Purchases	1,500

2. If the account contains only one entry, insert the figure required to make the account balance on the opposite side and label it *Balance c/f*. This is the balance carried forward at the end of the period (in this case, at the end of July). Insert

the same balancing figure on the same side as the original entry and label it *Balance b/f*. This is the balance brought forward at the start of the next period (in this case, at the start of August). The vehicle account is an example of this.

Vehicle account

		£			£
2 July	Bank	4,000	31 July	Balance c/f	4,000
1 August	Balance b/f	4,000			

3. If the account contains a number of entries, add up both sides. If both sides are the same, insert the totals and double underline them (there is no outstanding balance). An extension of the trade receivables account for Pippa Merton is an example of this.

Pippa Merton account

		£			£
2 July	Sales	2,800	20 July	Bank	750
5 July	Sales	200	28 July	Bank	2,550
12 July	Sales	300			
		3,300			3,300

4. If the two sides are not equal, use the larger figure as the total for both sides and insert the balancing figure on the side that originally had the smaller total. Complete the entry by bringing forward the balancing figure on the opposite side to become the opening balance for the next period. The bank account is an example of this.

Bank account

		£			£
1 July	Capital	10,000	1 July	Equipment	1,000
3 July	Sales	3,500	1 July	Purchases	4,000
12 July	Returns outward	200	1 July	Advertising	500
20 July	Pippa Merton	750	2 July	Car	4,000

(Continued)

		£			£
28 July	Pippa Merton	2,550	3 July	Purchases	2,000
			14 July	Returns inward	500
			28 July	Patel & Co	1,500
			31 July	Balance c/f	3,500
		17,000			17,000
1 August	Balance b/f	3,500			

Activity
Calculate the closing balances of the remaining accounts for Kool Kate Ltd: the capital account, the sales account, the purchases account, the equipment account, the returns inward account, the returns outward account and the advertising account.

You can check your answer in the next section where the closing balances are used to construct the trial balance.

When all the ledger accounts have been balanced off, some of them will have been closed completely, while others will show either a debit balance or a credit balance. A debit balance usually represents an asset or an expense, and a credit balance usually represents capital, revenue or liabilities. The list of debit and credit balances at the end of the accounting period is known as a *trial balance*. The total of the debit balances should be equal to the total of the credit balances. Some adjustments to the trial balance figures may be necessary to account for inventory, accruals, prepayments, depreciation and doubtful receivables after which the figures are used to prepare the financial statements. This is covered in subsequent chapters.

Definition
A trial balance is a listing of the balances on all the accounts of an organization, with debit balances in one column and credit balances in the other. If the rules of double-entry bookkeeping have been accurately applied, the totals of each column should be the same.

Source: Law, 2010, p. 420

Example

We can now calculate the closing balances on the accounts of Kool Kate Ltd at the end of the month and construct a trial balance. The debit balances are listed in the column on the left and the credit balances in the column on the right in the trial balance.

	Debit	Credit
Kool Kate Ltd		
Trial balance as at 31 July 2015		
	£	£
Capital at 1 July 2014		10,000
Sales revenue		6,800
Purchases	7,500	
Cash at bank	3,500	
Vehicles	4,000	
Equipment	1,000	
Returns inward	500	
Returns outward		200
Advertising	500	
	17,000	17,000
Note: Inventory at 31 July 2015 was £4,000		

When constructing a trial balance, it is usual to show the figure for closing inventory as a footnote because it is needed for preparing the financial statements. Kool Kate Ltd has *inventory* of £4,000 at the end of the month. This closing inventory of unsold goods becomes the opening inventory on the first day of the next accounting period.

Other transactions

Other common transactions include the following:

- *Carriage inward* refers to delivery charges for goods or materials purchased from suppliers. Sometime the business has to bear the cost of delivering its goods to customers, and this is known as *carriage outward*. Both are expenses and are shown in the debit column of the trial balance.

- When a business offers a cash discount to customers for prompt payment, it is referred to in the supplier's accounts as *discounts allowed*. It is an expense and is shown in the debit column of the trial balance. When a business receives cash discounts from its suppliers it is referred to in the customer's accounts as *discounts received* and is shown in the credit column of the trial balance.
- As well as maintaining a bank account, a business may keep a very small amount of cash known as *petty cash* for paying minor expenses. A cash account is an asset and is shown in the debit column of the trial balance. The balance shown on the ledger account for *bank* transactions appears in the debit column of the trial balance if the business has cash at the bank, because it is an asset. However, if the balance at the bank is an overdraft, it appears in the credit column of the trial balance because it is a liability.
- In addition to revenue arising from the sale of goods and services, a business may have other income in the form of interest, royalties and dividends. It is important that these items are recorded separately. They are not included with sales revenue. All items of revenue are shown in the credit column of the trial balance.

These transactions are dealt with in the usual way: each transaction is classified, an account is opened and the principles of double-entry bookkeeping are applied.

2.6   LIMITATIONS OF A TRIAL BALANCE

A trial balance can only detect arithmetical errors because it is simply a list of the debit balances and credit balances on the ledger accounts at the end of the accounting period. If the principles of double-entry bookkeeping have been followed, with a debit entry for every credit entry, the sum of the debit column in the trial balance will be the same as the sum of the credit column. If they do not balance, checks must be made to identify the reasons for any discrepancies. Common errors include:

- Transposing numbers – for example writing £320 instead of £230. To check for this error, calculate the difference between the total of the debit and credit columns on the trial balance. If this figure is divisible by 9, you have probably transposed a number somewhere.
- Omission – the transaction has not been recorded in the accounts at all.

- Wrong account – the transaction has been recorded in the wrong account (for example, in the vehicles account instead of the equipment account or in an asset account instead of a liability account).
- Wrong amount – the transaction has been recorded in the correct accounts, but the wrong amount was entered.
- Reverse entry – the transaction has been recorded in the correct accounts, but on the wrong side of both accounts.

The accuracy of the records in the accounting system is important, because they are used as the basis for preparing financial statements which summarise the transactions that have taken place during the accounting period. This period is usually one year.

2.7   KEY POINTS

Double-entry bookkeeping is the most efficient and effective method for recording transactions and events in a way that allows the balances on each ledger account at the end of the accounting period to be summarised in a trial balance. The trial balance acts as a check on the mathematical accuracy of the record keeping. However, there are some limitations as it does not show when transactions have been omitted and other errors that can occur. The trial balance is used as the basis for preparing the financial statements which summarise the transactions that have taken place during the accounting period.

REVISION QUESTIONS

1. David Green started Green Landscaping Ltd with £50,000 he inherited from his uncle. On 1 June he opened a bank account for the business and paid in the capital he has invested in the business. On the same day he wrote business cheques to buy a lorry for £16,000, to pay £1,400 to insure the lorry and to pay £4,500 for three months' rent on premises in advance. On 2 June he wrote three business cheques: £5,400 to pay for equipment, £850 to pay for materials from Timber Supplies Ltd and £420 to pay for advertising expenses. On 4 June the business bought a further £120 of materials on credit from Timber Supplies Ltd.

Required
Write up the ledger accounts for Green Landscaping Ltd.

2. Mrs Lesley owns a gift shop called Inspirational Ideas. On 4 July the cash account looked like this:

Cash account

		£			£
1 July	Opening balance	500	1 July	Postage	25
2 July	Cash sales	138	1 July	Window cleaning	10
3 July	Cash sales	192	1 July	Stationery	15
			1 July	Parking	2
			1 July	Stationery	36
			1 July	Petrol	18
			2 July	Parking	2
			2 July	Postage	31
			2 July	Purchases	104
			3 July	Parking	2
			3 July	Petrol	18
			3 July	Purchases	89

Required

Write up the ledger accounts for Inspirational Ideas to show the corresponding entries.

3. The following bank account shows transactions for Bristol Books Ltd for the month of October.

Bank account

		£			£
1 October	Balance b/f	6,400	2 October	Purchases	750
12 October	Sales	1,800	3 October	Advertising	1,120
15 October	Jones Ltd	950	16 October	Purchases	2,300
18 October	Jones Ltd	950	18 October	Davies Ltd	780
30 October	Sales revenue	1,450	25 October	Purchases	3,400

Required

Balance the account at 31 October and show the balance c/f at 1 November.

4. The following list of balances at 30 June 2015 is taken from the accounts of the Good Food Shop.

	£
Revenue	26,200
Purchases	?
Returns inward	900
Returns outward	460
Discounts allowed	720
Discounts received	620
Equipment	2,000
Bank	1,500
Salaries	1,600
Rent	1,400
General expenses	390
Capital at 1 July 2014	18,000

Required

Calculate the figure for purchases and prepare a trial balance at 30 June 2015 for the Good Food Shop.

5. Explain the advantages of a double-entry bookkeeping system and the purpose of a trial balance. In addition, discuss the limitations of a trial balance, giving examples to illustrate your answer.

3
FINANCIAL REPORTING FRAMEWORKS

3.1 OBJECTIVES

This chapter introduces the fundamental accounting principles for financial accounting and the regulatory and conceptual frameworks that underpin statutory financial reporting by limited liability entities in the UK. After studying this chapter, you should be able to:

- Explain the fundamental accounting principles.
- Describe the key elements of the regulatory framework for financial reporting.
- Explain the need for international convergence in financial reporting practices.
- Discuss the key principles of the IASB's Conceptual Framework for Financial Reporting.
- Define the elements of financial statements and the criteria for their recognition and measurement.

3.2 FUNDAMENTAL ACCOUNTING PRINCIPLES

In Chapter 1 we explained that *financial accounting* is primarily concerned with communicating a true and fair view of the financial performance and financial position of an entity to external parties at the end of the accounting period. Financial accounting has its roots in best practice in large listed companies, from which a number of *accounting principles* developed. Some of these concepts and conventions continue to shape financial accounting and financial reporting practices in businesses of all sizes.

Definition
Accounting principles are the basic theoretical concepts that guide financial accounting and financial reporting.

Source: Collis, Holt and Hussey, 2012, p. 23

Going concern

An underlying assumption is that financial statements are normally prepared on a going concern basis. The *going concern concept* is based on the principle that the entity will continue in operation for the foreseeable future. Therefore, unless it is known otherwise, it is assumed that the entity is not intending to close down or significantly reduce its activities. If that presumption is not valid, the financial statements will need to show the assets of the business at their break-up value and any liabilities that are applicable on liquidation (IASB, 2010a). Management must look at least 12 months ahead and, if there is significant doubt over the entity's ability to continue as a going concern, those uncertainties must be disclosed, together with the basis used (IASB, 2011a).

Activity

A company bought computer equipment at the beginning of the year for £6,000. It is estimated that it will contribute to the profits of the business for the next 3 years. Due to rapid changes in technology, six months later the chief accountant finds out that it would be worth only £1,000 if it had to be sold. Using the going concern concept, which of these two amounts should be shown in the accounts?

If the company is a going concern and will operate for the foreseeable future, it is anticipated that the equipment will continue to be used to contribute to the profit of the business. Therefore the correct answer is that it will be shown in the accounts at cost (£6,000). If the company is closing down, it must prepare the financial statements on a *break-up basis*. Therefore, the equipment would be shown at the estimated market value of the machine (£1,000). If there was no going concern concept, either of these figures might be used, which would be very confusing for users of the financial information.

A wide range of stakeholders in the company will be interested in whether it is a going concern. For example, if it is intending to close down or significantly reduce its activities:

- Existing investors would try to sell their shares and potential investors would be deterred from investing in the company.
- Existing lenders would demand repayment of loans, increase interest rates on overdraft facilities or even withdraw such facilities.
- Suppliers would be unwilling to supply goods and services on credit.
- Customers would be anxious about the continuity of supply of goods and services and switch to alternative providers. They would also be concerned if they

have bought goods that are still under warranty or those that require specialist replacement parts.
• Employees will be concerned about their job security, remuneration and future benefits.

Accrual accounting

A second underlying assumption is that, apart from cash flow information, financial statements are prepared using the accrual basis of accounting. The *accruals concept* is the principle that revenue and costs are recognised as they are earned and incurred, not as cash is received or paid (the *realisation concept*), and that they are matched with one another (the *matching concept*) and dealt with in the income statement of the period to which they relate (the time *period concept*). Under the accrual basis of accounting, the effects of economic transactions and events are shown in the period in which they occur, even if the resulting cash receipts and payments occur in a different period. In cash accounting, transactions and events are only recognised when cash has been received or paid.

Example
During the month of August a car dealer sold a vehicle for £7,500 that he had purchased at the beginning of the month for only £6,000. He paid cash for the car, but has not yet received the cash from the buyer. Using the accruals concept, we can calculate the profit he has made during the month as revenue minus purchases. As you can see, we are following the standard practice of using brackets to indicate figures that will be subtracted in the calculation:

	£
Revenue	7,500
Purchases	(6,000)
Profit	1,500

At the end of the month he has £6,000 less than he had at the start of the month because he has paid for the car, but has not yet received the cash from the buyer. We can show his cash position as follows:

	£
Cash at the start of the month	6,000
Purchases	(6,000)
Cash at the end of the month	0

It is because of the accruals concept that we need to use more than one financial statement to give a complete picture of the financial performance and wealth of a business. We will be looking at these financial statements in subsequent chapters.

Other fundamental accounting principles

In addition to the going concern concept and the accruals concept, you need to learn several other fundamental accounting principles at this stage.

- The *business entity concept* is the principle that the financial statements reflect the economic activities of the entity and not those of the owner(s). This means that the accounting records for a business must be kept separately from the personal accounting records of the owner.
- The *money measurement concept* is the principle that transactions are only recognised in the financial statements if they can be measured in monetary terms. Related to this concept is the assumption that currency is stable and holds its value over time (for example, there is no inflation or deflation and no fluctuations in foreign exchange rates).
- The *materiality concept* is the principle that only items of information that are material (significant) are included in the financial statements. An item of information is material if its omission or misstatement could influence the economic decisions of those using the financial statements.
- The *historical cost concept* is the principle that the values of assets are based on their original acquisition cost, unadjusted for subsequent changes in price or value. Historical cost is widely used, but is usually combined with *fair value*. The four main bases of fair value are current cost, net realisable value (selling price less costs of selling), value in use and replacement cost.
- The *consistency concept* is the principle of consistency in the accounting treatment of items of a similar nature within each accounting period and from one period to the next.
- The *prudence concept* is the principle that revenue and profits should be included only if there is reasonable certainty they will be received. However, provision for all known expenses and losses must be made, whether the amount is known with certainty or is a best estimate based on the information available. In other words, prudence is neither overstating assets nor understating liabilities under conditions of uncertainty. This is controversial because it conflicts with the notion that the financial statements need to be free from bias to give a faithful representation of the underlying transactions.

Figure 3.1 summarises the accounting principles we have discussed.

Figure 3.1 Fundamental accounting principles

3.3   THE REGULATORY FRAMEWORK FOR FINANCIAL REPORTING

Although financial accounting is guided by established accounting principles, over the years it has been found necessary to develop a *regulatory framework for financial reporting* to ensure that the financial statements are prepared in a standard way and provide high quality, reliable information for external users. Financial reporting is a key part of financial accounting. It refers to the statutory disclosure of general purpose financial information by limited liability entities via the *annual report and accounts*. The annual report and accounts contains narrative reports (such as the directors' report on the activities and operations throughout the year, and the auditors' report) and financial statements (the annual accounts). It is the most useful source of financial and other information issued by private and public companies.

> **Definition**
> Financial reporting refers to the statutory disclosure of general purpose financial information by limited liability entities via the annual report and accounts.
>
> Source: Collis, Holt and Hussey, 2012, p. 16

Voluntary disclosures may include information about the company's products, employees and corporate social responsibilities. There is some debate over the extent to which some of this information clutters the annual report, obscuring relevant information and making it harder for users to find the main points about the performance of the business and its future prospects. *Environmental and social reporting* is 'the process of communicating the social and environmental effects of organizations' economic activities to particular interest groups within society and to society at large. As such, it involves extending the accountability of organisations (particularly companies) beyond the traditional role of providing a financial account to the owners … [based on] the assumption that companies do have wider responsibilities than simply making money for their shareholders' (Gray, Owen and Maunders, 1987, p. ix).

The *Companies Act 2006 (Strategic Report and Directors' Reports) Regulations 2013* requires quoted companies to report on greenhouse gas emissions for which they are responsible in their annual report and accounts. In addition, they must report on environmental matters to the extent necessary for an understanding of the company's business, including key performance indicators (where appropriate). If this information is not disclosed, the annual report must point out the omissions. However, it can be argued that separate financial, environmental and corporate responsibility reports within the annual report and accounts can only provide a partial picture of how the entity adds economic, social, environmental value. This has led to demand for an integrated report capable of giving a holistic view in a concise, comparable format.

Small companies are often owner-managed, but in large companies there is separation of ownership and control and the annual report and accounts allows investors and other users to assess the financial performance, financial position and changes in financial position of the entity. Users rely on the integrity and judgement of the directors to provide high quality information. In companies that are not owner-managed, the directors are accountable to the investors and the information in the annual report and accounts allows the investors to assess the *stewardship* of the directors; in other words, the information helps investors assess how effectively and efficiently the directors have discharged their responsibilities in managing the business on their behalf.

> **Definition**
> Stewardship is a traditional approach to accounting that placed an obligation on stewards or agents, such as directors, to provide relevant and reliable financial information relating to the resources over which they have control but which are owned by others, such as shareholders.
>
> Source: Law, 2010, p. 398

One way in which the investors can trust that the financial statements the directors have prepared are a fair representation of the economic activities of the entity is to have the accounts audited. The auditors' report must include an opinion on whether the financial statements give a *true and fair view* of the company's profit or loss for the accounting period and of its state of affairs at the end of the period. There is no legal definition of a true and fair view, but essentially 'true' means the financial statements are in accordance with the facts (accurately reflect the underlying transactions) and 'fair' means they are not misleading. The auditors' report must also state whether the financial statements have been prepared consistently using appropriate accounting policies that are in accordance with company law and accounting standards. In addition, it must state whether there is adequate disclosure of information relevant to the proper understanding of the financial statements.

> **Definition**
> An audit is an independent examination of, and the subsequent expression of opinion on, the financial statements of an organization. This involves the auditor in collecting evidence by means of compliance tests (tests of control) and substantive tests (tests of detail).
>
> Source: Law, 2010, p. 37

The term *Generally Accepted Accounting Practice (GAAP)* refers to the regulatory framework for financial reporting that applies in a particular jurisdiction, hence the terms Indian GAAP, People's Public of China (PRC) GAAP, UK GAAP, US GAAP and so on. The key elements of UK GAAP are:

- Company law, which is developed by the government and sanctioned by Parliament.
- Accounting standards, which are issued by an independent (non-government) organisation.
- Stock exchange rules, which are issued by an independent regulator.

A detailed discussion of stock exchange rules is beyond the scope of this book. It is sufficient for you to know that the London Stock Exchange (LSE) is regulated independently by the *Financial Conduct Authority*. Public companies must meet stringent requirements to obtain a listing on LSE; less information is required for a listing on the *Alternative Investment Market (AIM)*, which is a subsidiary market for small, growing public companies. We will now look at company law and accounting standards in more detail.

3.4 COMPANY LAW

Company law in the UK is embodied in the *Companies Act 2006 (CA2006)* and subsequent statutory instruments that keep it up to date. It incorporates the requirements of EU Accounting Directives developed by the European Commission. Responsibility for developing company law rests with the Department for Business, Innovation and Skills (BIS), but it is enacted by Parliament.

The requirement to make the annual report and accounts available at a registry is based on the rationale that anyone dealing with a limited liability company should be able to see the financial statements. The official Registrar of Companies operates under the name of *Companies House*, which is an executive agency of BIS. Companies House has responsibility for incorporating and dissolving limited companies, examining and storing company information delivered under CA2006 and other related legislation, and making that information available to the public. On formation the company must register three documents:

- The *memorandum of association* defines the company's constitution and provides a record of facts at the time of incorporation. There is no need to state the objects of the company; hence no restriction on its activities.
- The *articles of association* is a document that gives details about the internal regulation of the business, including the voting rights of shareholders, how shareholders' and directors' meetings will be conducted and the powers of management. This is the core document approved by members that gives directors their operational parameters.
- The *statement of capital* provides information on the number of shares issued and the company's share capital.

CA2006 sets the general regulatory framework for financial reporting. The directors are required to prepare annual financial statements that comply with company law (including the form and content) and International Financial Reporting Standards (where applicable); additional information must be disclosed in the notes to the accounts. These annual accounts must be accompanied by a *directors' report*, signed by a director or company secretary. The directors must not approve the accounts unless they are satisfied that they give a *true and fair view* of the assets, liabilities, financial position and profit or loss. The annual accounts must also be accompanied by an *auditors' report*, signed by the auditors. The auditors' report consists of an opinion on whether the accounts show a true and fair view of the financial performance and position of the business.

Originally, the focus of UK GAAP was on financial reporting by large entities such as large single entities and groups (*Big GAAP*), but over the years a number of options have been introduced that simplify the requirements for smaller entities (*Little GAAP*). Under CA2006, unless the entity is excluded for reasons of public interest,[1] it will generally qualify as micro, small or medium if it meets two or more of three size criteria shown in Table 3.1 in its first year. Subsequently, it must satisfy the size tests in that year and the preceding year.

All these size groups must prepare full accounts for their shareholders, but small entities have the option of filing abbreviated accounts, if approved by all the company's directors, and there are fewer disclosures for micro-entities. Medium-sized entities can choose to file the slightly fuller version of abbreviated accounts that apply to them. Only small and micro-entities are exempt from the statutory requirement to have the accounts audited, but they cannot choose exemption if shareholders holding at least 10% of issued share capital require the accounts to be audited. At the time of writing (June 2015), the audit exemption thresholds were expected to rise to the levels shown in Table 3.1.

Table 3.1 Financial reporting size thresholds from 1 January 2016

Criteria	Micro	Small	Medium
Turnover	£0.632m	£10.2m	£36m
Balance sheet total	£0.316m	£5.1m	£18m
Average number of employees	10	50	250

Source: BIS, 2014c, pp. 18–19

---

[1] Under CA2006, 'an entity is excluded from the small companies regime if it is a public company, a company that is an authorised insurance company, a banking company, an e-money issuer, an ISD investment firm or a UCITS management company, or carries on insurance market activity, or is a member of an ineligible group' (c. 46, Part 15, Chapter 1, p. 178).

3.5   ACCOUNTING STANDARDS

Accounting standards provide preparers of financial statements with an authoritative guide to the most appropriate method for accounting for many of the important activities undertaken by companies. They apply to all entities that prepare financial statements intended to provide a true and fair view.

> **Definition**
> An accounting standard is an authoritative statement on how a particular type of transaction or other event should be reflected in the financial statements. In the UK, compliance with accounting standards is normally necessary for the financial statements to give a true and fair view.
>
> Source: Collis, Holt and Hussey, 2012, p. 99

Accounting standards provide users of financial statements with more information than is required by legislation alone. Users also have information about the basis on which the financial statements have been drawn up, which aids comparison with previous years and with other companies.

> **Activity**
> What do you think are the main disadvantages of accounting standards?

One of the disadvantages of accounting standards is that they impose additional compliance costs, but to some extent this is offset by the availability of accounting software. They also present a challenge for standard setters who must decide which accounting methods are appropriate for all companies in all industries and in all circumstances.

Not surprisingly, there are differences in the way countries have developed their regulatory frameworks for financial reporting due to a number of social, economic, legal and cultural reasons. This has resulted in significant differences in accounting practices. For example, some countries in the developing world have minimal financial reporting regulations, while other countries, such as the USA, have highly developed and prescriptive systems.

International differences in accounting standards mean that a company can show one figure of profit when the financial statements are drawn up under one country's rules and a completely different figure when drawn up under another country's rules. These differences are important when a company is seeking a listing on a stock exchange in another country. For example, if a UK company wanted its shares to be traded on the New York Stock Exchange as well as on the London Stock Exchange, it would need to prepare two sets of accounts. This is confusing for users and costly for the company, which must prepare one set of accounts that comply with US GAAP and another set that complies with UK GAAP.

Many businesses now have international operations thanks to the cross-border integration of markets and politics, and this has led to a demand for a single set of global accounting standards. The *IFRS Foundation* is the independent, not-for-profit private sector organisation responsible for developing *International Financial Reporting Standards (IFRSs)* through its standard setting body, the *International Accounting Standards Board (IASB)*. The IASB has also adopted some of the International Accounting Standards (IASs) issued by its predecessor, which still carry this name. IASs and IFRSs bring about convergence by reducing international differences in accounting practices. IFRSs are now required or permitted in more than 120 countries for all or some domestically listed companies.

The independent regulator in the UK with responsibility for promoting high standards of corporate governance and setting standards for financial reporting, auditing and actuarial practice is the *Financial Reporting Council (FRC)*. The FRC also contributes to the work of the IASB. For many years, the UK issued its own individual financial reporting standards (FRSs), but today UK GAAP is based on EU-adopted IFRSs. The following list of the UK's *Financial Reporting Standards (FRSs)* reflects this change:

- FRS 100, *Application of Financial Reporting Requirements* (2012) determines which reporting framework applies to which entities. Listed group entities have been required to use IFRSs since 2005.
- FRS 101, *Reduced Disclosure Framework* (2012) allows subsidiaries in a listed group to use IFRSs, but with fewer disclosures.
- FRS 102, *The Financial Reporting Standard Applicable in the UK and Republic of Ireland* (2013) is based on the IFRS for SMEs. It is a single standard that replaces all previously used UK accounting standards and is applicable to the remaining population of large, medium and small companies.
- FRS 105, *The Financial Reporting Standard Applicable to the Micro-Entities Regime* applies to micro-entities from 1 January 2016. The recognition and measurement requirements are based on FRS 102 with a number of significant simplifications. These include exempting micro-entities from having to account for complex transactions such as equity-settled share-based payments, defined benefit pension schemes and deferred tax. It can be used by micro-entities (as defined by the Companies Act 2006) which choose to apply the micro-entities regime introduced

in UK company law in November 2013. Micro-entities will only need to provide the disclosures required by law. At the time of writing (June 2015), the consultation on FRS 105 had not been completed, but there were indications that it will replace the *Financial Reporting Standard for Smaller Entities (FRSSE)*, which had been a choice for small companies since 1997.

By requiring the use of accounting standards based on IFRS, the UK has contributed to the reduction of international differences in financial accounting and reporting practices.

3.6   THE CONCEPTUAL FRAMEWORK FOR FINANCIAL REPORTING

The development of IFRSs is guided by the *Conceptual Framework for Financial Reporting* (IASB, 2010a). The Framework is not an IFRS, but a set of principles that underpin the preparation of *general purpose* financial statements. General purpose financial statements are those intended to meet the needs of a range of external users. They can be contrasted with *special purpose* financial statements, which are prepared for specific uses, such as share offerings, borrowing or tax purposes.

The purpose of the Framework is to:

- Assist the IASB in the development of future IFRSs and in its review of existing IFRSs.
- Assist the IASB in promoting harmonisation of regulations, accounting standards and procedures relating to the presentation of financial statements by providing a basis for reducing the number of alternative accounting treatments permitted by IFRSs.
- Assist national standard setting bodies in developing national standards.
- Assist preparers of financial statements in applying IFRSs and in dealing with topics that have yet to form the subject of an IFRS.
- Assist auditors in forming an opinion on whether financial statements comply with IFRSs.
- Assist users of financial statements in interpreting the information contained in financial statements prepared in compliance with IFRSs.
- Provide those who are interested in the work of the IASB with information about its approach to the formulation of IFRSs.

> **Definition**
> A conceptual framework is a statement of theoretical principles that provides guidance for financial accounting and reporting.
>
> Source: Law, 2010, p. 102

Objective of general purpose financial reporting

The Framework states that the *objective* of general purpose financial reporting is to provide information about the reporting entity that is useful to existing and potential investors, lenders and other creditors in making decisions about providing resources to the entity. Those decisions involve buying, selling or holding equity and debt instruments and providing or settling loans and other forms of credit. This principle forms the foundation of the Framework and other aspects of the Framework flow logically from it. Figure 3.2 summarises the needs of the primary user groups.

The Framework acknowledges that general purpose financial reports cannot meet all the information needs of the primary users, many of whom are not in a position to demand special purpose financial reports. Therefore, they will also need to obtain information from other sources such as reports on general economic conditions and expectations, political events and political climate, and industry and company outlooks. For example, if you were an investor, you could make use of information supplied by investment analysts or conduct your own analysis of the economy from

Figure 3.2 Primary users of general purpose financial reports

International Monetary Fund reports. You could analyse the industry from market reports and compare the entity's performance against that of its competitors or industry benchmarks using data from trade associations or financial databases.

> **Activity**
> The IASB's Framework focuses on the primary user groups. Who are the other significant users of general purpose financial reports and what are their information needs?

You may have thought of the following groups:

- Employees need information for assessing any immediate financial benefits, such as a bonus based on the company's results, or for pay bargaining. They are also interested in information that helps them assess any risk to their job security, future prospects or future benefits, such as private health insurance and retirement pension.
- Customers are interested in information about the continued existence of the business and its ability to supply goods and services, especially if there are product warranties or specialised replacement parts involved.
- The government and its agencies are interested in the allocation of resources and the effect of their economic and fiscal policies. Therefore, they need information for regulatory purposes, assessing taxation and compiling statistics.
- The public in general are interested in information that is relevant to how they are affected by the company. For example, the contribution it makes to the local economy by providing employment or using local suppliers; its involvement in the community; its contributions to political and charitable groups; its sustainability policies and impact on the environment.

The Framework notes that the needs of *management* are not considered because managers can obtain the information they need internally. Although other external parties, including *regulators* and members of the *public* may also find general purpose financial reports useful, such reports are not directed at meeting their specific needs.

Investors, lenders and other creditors have a common interest in information about the entity's economic resources and the claims against the reporting entity. This information is shown in the *statement of financial position* (also known as the balance sheet). They are also interested in information about the effects of transactions and other events that change a reporting entity's economic resources and claims. This is shown in the *statement of comprehensive income* (also known as the profit and loss account). Finally, they have a common interest in the changes in the entity's cash flows, which are presented in the *statement of cash flows*. However, one point of difference is that lenders and major suppliers have the economic power to demand special purpose financial statements, but investors have no such power and must rely on general purpose financial statements.

Qualitative characteristics of usefulness

The first principle of the Framework is that the objective of financial reporting is to provide information that is useful to users. Chapter 3 of the Framework (IASB, 2010a) identifies further accounting principles by dividing the *qualitative character-istics* that are likely to make the financial information useful into *fundamental* and *enhancing* characteristics. These accounting principles apply to financial information provided in financial statements, as well as to financial information provided in other ways.

The fundamental qualitative characteristics are:

- *Relevance* – Relevant financial information is capable of making a difference to users' decisions. Financial information is capable of making a difference to deci-sions if it has predictive value and/or confirmatory value. These two are interre-lated. *Materiality* is an entity-specific aspect of relevance based on the nature or magnitude (or both) of the items to which the information relates in the context of an individual entity's financial report. The *materiality concept* is the principle that only items of information that are material (significant) are included in the financial statements. An item of information is material if its omission or misstate-ment could influence the economic decisions of those using the financial state-ments. Materiality depends on the size of the item or error and the circumstances of its omission or misstatement (for example, an omission of revenue of £10 versus an omission of £10,000).
- *Faithful representation* – General purpose financial reports represent economic phenomena in words as well as numbers. To be useful, the information must not only represent relevant phenomena but it must also be a faithful representation of the phenomena. Ideally it should be complete, neutral and free from error. Free from error does not mean perfectly accurate. For example, an estimate of an unobservable value cannot be perfectly accurate, but it is a faithful representation if it is clearly described as being an estimate and the nature and limitations of the estimating process are explained, and no errors have been made in selecting and applying an appropriate process for developing the estimate.

Subject to the effects of enhancing characteristics and the cost constraint, the Framework suggests that the most efficient and effective process for applying the fundamental qualitative characteristics would usually be:

1. Identify an economic phenomenon that has the potential to be useful to users of the reporting entity's financial information.
2. Identify the type of information about that phenomenon that would be most relevant if it is available and can be faithfully represented.
3. Determine whether that information is available and can be faithfully represented. If so, the process of satisfying the fundamental qualitative characteristics ends at that point. If not, the process is repeated with the next most relevant type of information.

The Framework points out that the enhancing qualitative characteristics cannot make information useful if that information is irrelevant or it is not faithfully represented. The enhancing qualitative characteristics are:

- *Comparability* – The information is more useful if it can be compared with similar information for the entity in other periods, or similar information for other entities. A comparison requires at least two items. Consistency helps achieve comparability and refers to the use of the same methods for the same items, either from period to period within a reporting entity or in a single period across entities.
- *Verifiability* – The financial information is more useful if it is verifiable. Verifiability helps to assure users that the information is a faithful representation. It means that different knowledgeable and independent observers could reach consensus, although not necessarily complete agreement, that a particular depiction is a faithful representation.
- *Timeliness* – The financial information is more useful if it is timely. Timeliness means that information is available to users in time to be capable of influencing their decisions.
- *Understandability* – The financial information is more useful if it is readily understandable. Classifying, characterising and presenting information clearly and concisely makes it understandable. While some phenomena are inherently complex and cannot be made easy to understand, to exclude such information would make financial reports incomplete and potentially misleading. Financial reports are prepared for users who have a reasonable knowledge of business and economic activities and who review and analyse the information with diligence.

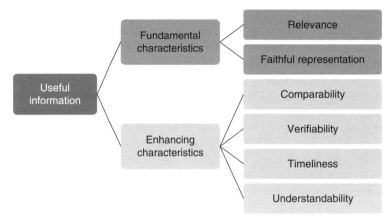

Figure 3.3 Qualitative characteristics of useful financial information

Figure 3.3 summarises the qualitative characteristics of usefulness we have discussed.

The following activity will help you think about some of the main qualitative characteristics that make financial information useful.

Activity

Think about your bank statements or credit card statement and answer the following questions:

	Yes	No
(a) Is any item insignificant or irrelevant?	❏	❏
(b) Does the information help you make spending or borrowing decisions?	❏	❏
(c) Is the information a faithful representation of your transactions?	❏	❏
(d) Is the information timely enough to make spending or borrowing decisions to stop you inadvertently incurring additional costs?	❏	❏
(e) Is the information prepared consistently so that you can compare it with corresponding information for previous periods?	❏	❏
(f) Assuming the information is relevant, is it easy to understand?	❏	❏

3.7   FINANCIAL STATEMENTS

Guidance on the presentation of general purpose financial statements is contained in IAS 1, *Presentation of Financial Statements* (IASB, 2011a). Table 3.2 compares the IAS 1 titles for the financial statements with those traditionally used in the UK. You need to remember that reporting entities can use other titles for the financial statements and the illustrative formats are not mandatory.

An entity must present a complete set of financial statements at least annually with notes that provide a summary of accounting policies and other explanatory information relating to the items in the financial statements. Comparative information for the previous period must also be provided. The following items must be identified:

- The reporting enterprise.
- Whether the statements are for a single entity or a group.
- The date or period covered.
- The presentation currency and the level of precision (thousands, millions, etc.).

Each material class of items must be presented separately in the financial statements and dissimilar items may be aggregated only if they are individually immaterial. For consistency, the presentation and classification of items in the financial statements should stay the same from one period to the next, unless a change is justified by a change in circumstances or a new IFRS (IAS 1, para 45).

We are now ready to consider the elements in the financial statements. The Framework explains that financial statements present the effects of economic transactions and other events in broad categories according to their economic characteristics, which form the elements of general purpose financial statements.

Table 3.2 Set of financial statements

IAS 1 terminology	Traditional UK terminology
Statement of comprehensive income	Profit and loss account
Statement of financial position	Balance sheet
Statement of changes in equity	Statement of recognised gains and losses
Statement of cash flows	Cash flow statement

Financial performance

Financial performance is concerned with the profitability of the entity. Users need information on the entity's financial performance to assess potential changes in its economic resources and its capacity to generate cash from its resources. In addition, users need information to evaluate how effectively any additional resources might be used. The elements that relate to the measurement of financial performance are shown in the *statement of comprehensive income* and the *statement of changes in equity*. These are:

- Income.
- Expenses.

Definitions

Income is increases in economic benefits during the accounting period in the form of inflows or enhancements of assets or decreases of liabilities that result in increases in equity, other than those relating to contributions from equity participants.

Expenses are decreases in economic benefits during the accounting period in the form of outflows or depletions of assets or incurrences of liabilities that result in decreases in equity, other than those relating to distributions to equity participants.

Source: IASB, 2010a, para 4.25

Under IAS 1 (IASB, 2011a) and the *IFRS for SMEs* (IASB, 2009a), income and expenses must not be offset against each other, unless expressly required or permitted. The Framework explains that the definition of income encompasses both *revenue* and *gains*. Revenue arises in the course of the ordinary activities of the business. Gains represent other items that meet the definition of income and may or may not arise in the course of the ordinary activities of an entity. As gains represent increases in economic benefits, they are no different in nature from other revenue and are not treated as a separate element [4.29–30]. The definition of expenses encompasses both *expenses* and *losses*. Expenses arise in the course of the ordinary activities of the business. Losses represent other items that meet the definition of expenses and may or may not arise in the course of the ordinary activities of an entity. As losses represent decreases in economic benefits, they are no different in nature from other expenses and are not treated as a separate element [4.33–34].

Financial position

Financial position is concerned with the economic resources the entity controls, its financial structure, its liquidity and solvency and its ability to adapt to changes in the business environment. Users need information on the entity's financial position to help them assess its ability to generate future cash flows and evaluate how those cash flows will be distributed among stakeholders. In addition, users need information to evaluate the entity's ability to raise any finance that might be needed and to meet financial commitments when they fall due. The elements that relate to the measurement of financial position are shown in the *statement of financial position*. These are:

- Assets.
- Liabilities.
- Equity.

Definitions

An asset is a resource controlled by the entity as a result of past events and from which future economic benefits are expected to flow to the entity.

A liability is a present obligation of the entity resulting from past events, the settlement of which is expected to result in an outflow from the entity of resources embodying economic benefits.

Equity is the residual interest in the assets of the entity after deducting all its liabilities.

Source: IASB, 2010a, para 4.4

Under IAS 1 (IASB, 2011a) and the *IFRS for SMEs* (IASB, 2009a), assets and liabilities must not be offset against each other, unless expressly required or permitted.

Recognition and measurement of elements

The Framework defines *recognition* as the process of incorporating in the statement of financial position or statement of comprehensive income an item that meets the definition of an element and satisfies the following criteria for recognition:

- It is probable that any future economic benefit associated with the item will flow to or from the entity.
- The item has a cost or value that can be measured with reliability [4.37–38].

Based on these general criteria:

- *Income* is recognised in the statement of comprehensive income when an increase in future economic benefits related to an increase in an asset or a decrease of a liability has arisen and can be measured reliably. Thus, the recognition of income occurs simultaneously with the recognition of an increase in an asset or a decrease of a liability.

- *Expenses* are recognised in the statement of comprehensive income when a decrease in future economic benefits related to a decrease in an asset or an increase of a liability has risen that can be measured reliably. Thus, the recognition of expenses occurs simultaneously with the recognition of an increase in a liability or a decrease in an asset.
- An *asset* is recognised in the statement of financial position when it is probable that the future economic benefits will flow to the entity and the asset has a cost or value that can be measured reliably.
- A *liability* is recognised in the statement of financial position when it is probable that an outflow of resources embodying economic benefits will result from the settlement of a present obligation and the amount at which the settlement will take place can be measured reliably.

The Framework defines measurement as the process of determining the monetary amounts at which the elements of the financial statements are to be recognised and carried in the statement of financial position and the statement of comprehensive income statement [4.54]. It is important to note that the Framework does not include principles for selecting the basis of measurement for particular elements of financial statements or in particular circumstances, but mentions the following four bases:

- *Historical cost* – Under historical cost, assets are recorded at the amount paid or the fair value of the consideration given at the time they were acquired. Liabilities are recorded at the amount of proceeds received in exchange for the obligation or at the amounts expected to be paid to satisfy the liability in the normal course of business.
- *Current cost* – Assets are carried at the amount of cash or cash equivalents that would have to be paid if the same or an equivalent asset was acquired currently. Liabilities are carried at the undiscounted amount of cash or cash equivalents that would be required to settle the obligation currently. From this you can see that current cost could be described as the replacement value or the entry value.
- *Realisable (settlement) value* – Assets are carried at the amount of cash or cash equivalents that could currently be obtained by selling the asset in an orderly disposal. Liabilities are carried at their settlement values, which are the undiscounted amounts to be paid to satisfy the liabilities in the normal course of business. From this you can see that realisable value represents the exit value.

• *Present value* – Assets are carried at the present discounted value of the future net cash inflows that the item is expected to generate in the normal course of business. Liabilities are carried at the present discounted value of the future net cash outflows that are expected to be required to settle the liabilities in the normal course of business.

3.8 KEY POINTS

Fundamental accounting principles guide the general process of financial accounting, but a regulatory framework is needed to ensure that financial statements are prepared in a standard way and provide high quality, reliable information. The regulatory framework for financial reporting has three main elements: company law, accounting standards and stock exchange rules. UK GAAP is now based on *International Financial Reporting Standards (IFRSs)*. The *Conceptual Framework for Financial Reporting* (IASB, 2010a) provides theoretical principles that underpin the development of IFRSs. We have examined the objective of financial reporting, the users of general purpose financial reports and the qualitative characteristics that make financial information useful. Guidance on the presentation of general purpose financial statements is contained in IAS 1, *Presentation of Financial Statements* (IASB, 2011a).

REVISION QUESTIONS

1. Describe the two underlying assumptions that underpin financial accounting and reporting, providing examples to illustrate your answer.
2. Describe the three key elements of the regulatory framework for financial reporting. In addition, explain how UK GAAP for listed and unlisted companies is now based on IFRSs.
3. Explain what an accounting standard is and discuss the need for international convergence in financial reporting practices.
4. Describe the objective of general purpose financial reporting and discuss the information needs of the three primary user groups identified in the IASB Framework (2010).
5. Discuss the qualitative characteristics of useful financial information.

4
STATEMENT OF COMPREHENSIVE INCOME

4.1 OBJECTIVES

Under IAS 1, *Presentation of Financial Statements* (IASB, 2011a), a complete set of financial statements includes a statement of comprehensive income. After studying this chapter, you should be able to:

- Explain the purpose of the statement of comprehensive income.
- Differentiate between accruals and prepayments.
- Calculate depreciation using the straight-line method.
- Differentiate between bad debts and doubtful receivables.
- Prepare a statement of comprehensive income.

4.2 PURPOSE OF THE STATEMENT OF COMPREHENSIVE INCOME

Users of general purpose financial statements (see Chapter 3) have a common interest in information about the effects of transactions and other events that change a reporting entity's economic resources and claims. This is shown in the *statement of comprehensive income*. The purpose of the statement of comprehensive income is to provide information to users on the financial performance of business over the accounting period (usually one year); in other words, the amount of the profit or loss the business has made during the period. Because it is retrospective, it is sometimes referred to as a financial history book. The elements that relate to the measurement of financial performance are *income* and *expenses*, which we defined in Chapter 2. Income includes both revenue and gains, and expenses include both costs and losses. A profit or loss is the difference between the income earned and expenses incurred over the period. One of the most important things to remember is that a profit or loss can be made whether the transactions of the business are for cash or on credit because the statement of comprehensive income is prepared on an accrual basis (see Chapter 3).

Activity

Imagine that you have £200 that you use to buy a computer for resale. You decide to advertise the computer, which costs £10, and you sell it for £300. However, the buyer is not able to pay you straight away, so you give him one month's credit. You have no other business transactions. Calculate your cash position at the end the month and your profit for the month.

It is likely that you have been able to work out the cash position in your head by deducting the total cash outflows from the total cash inflows. To calculate the profit, you need to deduct all the costs you incurred in the month from the value of the sale. If you have studied accounting before, you may have used the following layouts:

Your business	
Cash flow statement for the month	
	£
Cash inflows	
Capital	200
Cash outflows	
Purchases	200
Advertising	10
	(210)
Net cash flow	(10)

Your business	
Statement of comprehensive income for the month	
	£
Revenue	300
Cost of sales	
Purchases	(200)
Gross profit	100
Expenses	
Advertising	(10)
Profit for the period	90

The cash flow statement shows that the cash position is a deficit of £10. This might mislead you into thinking that you have made a loss of £10 (the cost you have incurred) or a loss of £300 (the amount owing to you). Neither figure is correct. The answer is a profit of £90. This is because you are using the principles of accrual accounting when calculating the profit or loss for the period. You need to remember that the statement of comprehensive income does not tell us anything about cash. For example, it does not tell us about the £200 capital; nor does it tell us whether cash has been received for the sale of the computer or the costs incurred by the business have been paid.

Looking at the terms used in our simple cash flow statement, *capital* describes the money contributed by the owner to enable the business to function. *Purchases* refers to cash flowing out of the business to suppliers in respect of goods bought for resale and *advertising* represents cash flowing out of the business when that expense is paid. However, in the statement of comprehensive income, *revenue* refers to all sales made to customers during the period (irrespective of whether cash has changed hands); *purchases* refers to the cost of goods purchased from suppliers for resale during the period (irrespective of whether cash has changed hands); and *advertising* refers to the total for that expense during the period (irrespective of whether cash has changed hands).

4.3   DRAFT STATEMENT OF COMPREHENSIVE INCOME

The first thing to determine when preparing a *statement of comprehensive income* is the accounting period over which the profit or loss will be calculated. As the financial statement will be prepared on an accrual basis, all sources of income for the period need to be included, irrespective of whether the transactions were for cash or on credit: in other words, irrespective of whether cash has been received yet. This revenue is then matched with the revenue expenditure, which are the costs and expenses incurred during the period in order to earn the income, irrespective of whether cash has been paid yet. The calculation of profit is based on the following equation:

Income – Expenses = Profit or loss for the period

Users of the financial statements of trading businesses need detailed information about the profit made on buying and selling goods, which is known as the *gross profit*. This is calculated as the difference between revenue for the period and the *cost of sales*. The cost of sales is the cost of the goods that have been sold during the period.

Revenue – Cost of sales = Gross profit

The term *gross* is used to describe the profit at this stage because this is the larger figure of profit before any of the overhead expenses have been deducted. If the business had any *other income* (such as interest received on investments or rent received from lettings) it would be shown after the figure for gross profit. The figure for *operating profit* is obtained by deducting *distribution costs* (such as packaging, postage, transport costs and insurance of goods in transit), *administrative expenses* (such as office rent, salaries, cleaning, telephone and stationery) and *other expenses* from gross profit. The distribution costs, administrative and other operating expenses are known collectively as *revenue expenditure*.

Gross profit – Revenue expenditure = Operating profit

Next, any finance costs (for example, interest paid on loans) are deducted separately to give the *profit before tax*. Income tax expense is then deducted to give the *profit for the year*. Finally, any holding gain made when an asset is sold is added to give the figure of *comprehensive income* that includes all profits and gains made over the accounting period.

Definitions

Gross profit is the difference between the revenue and the cost of goods sold during the period.

Operating profit is the difference between the operating income and revenue expenditure for the period.

Comprehensive income is the total of all profits and gains made over the period.

Source: Collis, Holt and Hussey, 2012, p. 134

Under IAS 1, *Presentation of Financial Statements* (IASB, 2011a) and the *IFRS for SMEs* (IASB, 2009b), reporting entities have two main choices regarding the statement of comprehensive income:

- Prepare a single *statement of comprehensive income* or the same information presented in two separate statements: an *income statement* showing components of profit or loss and a *statement of comprehensive income* that shows the components of other comprehensive income.
- Analyse expenses by nature or by function, whichever provides information that is relevant and more reliable. If expenses are analysed by function, information by nature must be disclosed in the notes to the financial statements.

Example

On 1 January 2015 Lily Zhang set up a business called Lily Soap Ltd selling boxes of luxury soap. She works from a small unit on an industrial estate near her home, buying soaps from local suppliers and selling them via a market stall and on the Internet. She has started the business with £10,000 capital and a bank loan of £6,500 for a period of two years. The loan has a fixed interest rate of 7.4% which works out at £40 per month.

The following table summarises the quantities and values of the purchases and sales of boxes of soap over the first six months.

Date	Purchases		Cash sales		Credit sales	
	Quantity	£	Quantity	£	Quantity	£
January	400	6,000	80	1,600	240	4,800
February	400	6,000	90	1,800	270	5,400
March	500	7,500	100	2,000	300	6,000
April	560	8,400	175	3,500	390	7,800
May	600	9,000	205	4,100	410	8,200
June	600	9,000	225	4,500	425	8,500
Total	3,060	45,900	875	17,500	2,035	40,700

Activity
(a) What was the revenue for the period?
(b) How many boxes of unsold soap did Lily Soaps Ltd have at the end of June and what was the total cost of that closing inventory?

The answer to (a) is calculated in Working 1:

Working 1	£
Cash sales	17,500
Credit sales	40,700
Revenue	58,200

To answer (b), you need to calculate the quantity of closing inventory. *Closing inventory* refers to the unsold goods at the end of the accounting period. A business needs to have a certain amount of goods in stock on the last day of the period to be able to sell them on the first day of the next period, which means closing inventory at the end of the period is *opening inventory* at the start of the next period. In order to value closing inventory, at the end of the accounting period (the maximum being one year), a physical count of goods is carried out to compare those quantities with the records. This is referred to as *stocktaking*. Once the total number of items in stock is known, the value is calculated by multiplying the number of items by the original cost of the item.

Value of closing inventory = Quantity of opening inventory + Quantity purchased
− Quantity sold

Lily Soaps Ltd had no opening inventory because this is the first six months of trading, so check your figures against Working 2:

Working 2	Quantity
Purchases	3,060
Cash sales	(875)
Credit sales	(2,035)
Closing inventory	150

The cost of sales is calculated as:

Value of opening inventory + Purchases − Closing inventory

Lily Soaps Ltd has no opening inventory, so we simply need to subtract the value of closing inventory from purchases as shown in Working 3:

Working 3	£
Purchases (£15 × 3,060)	45,900
Closing inventory (£15 × 150)	(2,250)
Cost of sales	43,650

We can now draft the trading section of the statement of comprehensive income.

Lily Soaps Ltd **Draft statement of comprehensive income** **for 6 months ended 30 June 2015**	
	£
Revenue (W1)	58,200
Cost of sales (W2 and W3)	(43,650)
Gross profit	14,550

As you can see, the company made a gross profit of £14,550 during the first six months and we can cross-check this by doing a small calculation. We know that the business buys each box of soap for £15 and sells it for £20 per box, thus making a gross profit of £5 per box. As 2,910 boxes have been sold in the period, the gross profit is £5 × 2,910 = £14,550. In a more complex business, you could not carry out these simple calculations.

The *cost of sales* reflects the cost of the goods sold. In this example we deducted the cost of the closing inventory from the cost of the goods purchased during the period. This is because we are preparing this financial statement on an *accrual* basis and want to match the revenue to the cost of purchasing the soap actually sold during the period. We are ignoring the movement of cash.

We now need to deduct the operating expenses for the period in order to calculate the operating profit. Rent was £3,000, advertising £300, telephone and Internet expenses were £900, printing, postage and stationery expenses were £500 and salaries were £5,320. We also need to consider any other expenses, such as income tax. Lily's accountant tells her this is expected to be £2,085. As Lily Soaps Ltd has no other income or gains, we now have everything we need to complete the draft statement of comprehensive income for the six months ended 30 June 2015.

Lily Soaps Ltd **Draft statement of comprehensive income** **for 6 months ended 30 June 2015**	
	£
Revenue (W1)	58,200
Cost of sales (W2 and W3)	(43,650)
Gross profit	14,550
Expenses	
Rent	(3,000)
Advertising	(300)
Telephone and Internet	(900)
Printing, postage and stationery	(500)
Salaries (£5,320 ÷ 2)	(2,660)
	(7,360)
Operating profit	7,190
Finance costs	(240)
Profit before tax	6,950
Income tax expense	(2,085)
Profit for the period	4,865

The draft statement of comprehensive income shows that the business made a *profit for the period* of £4,865. If the total expenses were greater than the total income the final figure would be negative and you would label it 'loss for the period'. Under the

IFRS for SMEs, if an entity has no items of other comprehensive income in any of the periods for which financial statements are presented, it is allowed to present an income statement alone or it can present a statement of comprehensive income in which the 'bottom line' is labelled profit (or loss), as Lily has done.

We will now look at how the statement of comprehensive income is prepared from a trial balance. Although the records in the accounting system may be fully up to date, it is always necessary to make a number of *post trial balance adjustments* (adjustments that are made after the trial balance has been generated) to ensure that the principles of the accruals concept are met. Here is the trial balance at 31 December 2015, which marks the end of the first year of trading for Lily Soaps Ltd. Note that the proportionately higher finance cost for the year (shown as 'interest on loan' in the trial balance) compared with the first six months reflects higher rates charged by the bank in the second half of the year.

	Debit	Credit
Lily Soaps Ltd		
Trial balance at 31 December 2015		
	£	£
Revenue		173,200
Purchases	113,400	
Equipment (at cost)	13,000	
Trade receivables	27,500	
Trade payables		15,000
Cash	26,100	
Salaries	14,500	
Rent	6,000	
Advertising	600	
Telephone & Internet	1,960	
Printing, postage & stationery	1,100	
Interest on loan	540	
Loan		6,500
Share capital at 1 January 2015		10,000
	204,700	204,700

4.4 INVENTORY, ACCRUALS AND PREPAYMENTS

Inventory

In a trading business, *inventory* refers to unsold goods, but in a manufacturing business, it comprises raw materials, work-in-progress and finished goods. IAS 2, *Inventories* (IASB, 2003a) and the *IFRS for SMEs* (IASB, 2009b) require inventory to be valued at the lower of cost or *net realisable value (NRV)*. Cost includes the purchase cost, conversion cost (materials, labour and overheads) and other costs (excluding foreign exchange differences) that are necessary to bring inventory to its present location and condition.

Definition
Net realisable value (NRV) is the sales value of the [inventory] less any additional costs likely to be incurred in getting the [inventories] into the hands of the customer.

Source: Law, 2010, p. 294

As mentioned earlier, the figure for inventory at the end of the period (closing inventory) is the figure for inventory at the start of the next period (opening inventory). In the statement of comprehensive income, the adjustments for opening and closing inventory are incorporated in the cost of sales calculation.

Activity
Total purchases during the year ended 31 December 2015 were £113,400. The annual stocktake at the end of the year showed that Lily Soaps Ltd had 50 boxes of soap in stock which had cost £15 each. What is the cost of sales for the year ended 31 December 2015?

Check your answer against Working 1.

Working 1	£
Purchases	113,400
Closing inventory (£15 × 50)	(750)
Cost of sales	112,650

Because of the impact of closing inventory on profit, this is an area where fraud can be perpetrated if adjustments are not made to take account of lost or damaged goods. Therefore, inventory is one of the key checks made by the auditors.

Accruals

When the ledger accounts are closed at the end of the accounting period, some expenses incurred for goods and services may not have been recorded because the business has not yet received an invoice or statement from the supplier. The business needs to estimate the amount of any accrued expense or liability and add the *accrual* to the trial balance figure for that expense because it belongs to the accounting period for which the financial statements are being prepared.

Definition

An accrual is an estimate of a liability that is not supported by an invoice or a request for payment at the time when the accounts are prepared.

Source: Law, 2010, p. 11

Lily Soaps Ltd has two accrued expenses:

- The trial balance shows telephone and Internet expenses of £1,960, but these only cover the first 11 months and the accountant Lily has employed estimates that a further £200 is owed for December. This means that the expense shown in the statement of comprehensive income should be £1,960 + £200 = £2,160.
- The accountant knows from the invoices for advertising that the total amount paid was £600, but during December Lily took out extra advertisements to promote sales over the festive season. The company will not be invoiced for these advertisements until January, but the accountant estimates the amount will be £100. This means that the expense shown in the statement of comprehensive income should be £600 + £100 = £700.

Prepayments

Another situation that commonly arises is when part of the amount paid for an expense in the current accounting period covers goods or services that will not be received until the next period. The amount of this payment in advance is known and the *prepayment* needs to be deducted from the trial balance figure for that expense.

Definition

A prepayment is a payment made for goods or services before they are received.

Source: Law, 2010, p. 328

Lily Soaps Ltd has one prepayment. Lily has recorded printing, postage and stationery expenses of £1,100 in the accounts, but at the end of December she realises that she has accumulated a small surplus of these items that the business will not use until January. The cost of these items was £100. This means that the expense shown in the statement of comprehensive income should be £1,100 − £100 = £1,000.

4.5 DEPRECIATION OF PROPERTY, PLANT AND EQUIPMENT

In Chapter 2 we defined an asset as a resource controlled by the entity as a result of past events and from which future economic benefits are expected to flow to the entity (IASB, 2010a, para 4.4). The cost of acquiring or producing the asset (for example, buying components and building a new computer system), or enhancing an existing asset (for example, extending or refurbishing a factory or office building) is classified as *capital expenditure*. This does not concern us here as we are focusing on revenue expenditure.

IAS 16, *Property, Plant and Equipment* (IASB, 2008) and the *IFRS for SMEs* (IASB, 2009b) give guidance on the accounting treatment of certain *tangible non-current assets* that include freehold and leasehold land, buildings, fixtures and fittings, machinery, equipment and delivery vehicles. Tangible assets are non-monetary in nature and have a physical substance. They can be distinguished from *intangible non-current assets* that do not have a physical form, such as goodwill, patents and trademarks.

Definition

Property, plant and equipment are tangible assets that are held for use in the production of supply of goods or services, for rental to others, or for administrative purposes, and are expected to be used during more than one period.

Source: IAS 16, para 7 (IASB, 2008)

Under IAS 16, all items of property, plant and equipment (PPE) with a finite life must be depreciated. *Depreciation* is the systematic allocation of the cost or revalued amount of a tangible non-current asset, less any residual value, over its useful life. Thus, depreciation represents the consumption of the economic benefits embodied in the asset. The asset's *useful life* is an estimate of the number of years it is expected to be available for use by the entity or the number of production or similar units expected to be obtained from the asset by the entity. Some assets, such as fixtures and fittings or vehicles will be worn out after a period of time; others, such as machinery or equipment, are likely to become obsolete through advances in technology. On the basis of materiality, some entities write off low value items to expenses in the year of purchase (for example, equipment that cost £250 or less).

> **Definitions**
>
> Depreciation is the systematic allocation of the depreciable amount of an asset over its useful life.
>
> The depreciable amount is the cost of an asset, or other amount substituted for cost, less its residual value.
>
> Residual value is the estimated amount that an entity would currently obtain from disposal of the asset, after deducting the estimated costs of disposal, if the asset were already of the age and in the condition expected at the end of its useful life.
>
> Useful life is the period over which an asset is expected to be available for use by an entity ... or the number of production or similar units expected to be obtained from the asset by the entity.
>
> Source: IAS 16, para 6 (IASB, 2008)

An *allowance for depreciation* is made for each category of PPE in order to match the revenue the asset has helped generate during the accounting period to an estimate of the cost that has been consumed during the year.

The cost of an item of property, plant and equipment is recognised as an asset only if:

(a) It is probable that future economic benefits associated with the item will flow to the entity.
(b) The cost of the item can be measured reliably.

Under the *IFRS for SMES*, initial recognition is at cost. In subsequent years, recognition is at cost less any accumulated depreciation and any accumulated impairment losses. Under IAS 16, the initial measurement is also at cost, but in subsequent years two measurement models are offered:

• The *cost model*, where the asset is carried at cost less accumulated depreciation and accumulated impairment losses (the same as under the *IFRS for SMEs*).
• The *revaluation model*, where the asset is carried at a revalued amount, being its fair value at the date of revaluation less subsequent accumulated depreciation and impairment, provided that fair value can be measured reliably.

The model chosen must be applied consistently across the class of assets (for example, for all equipment).

Table 4.1 Examples of fair value

Asset	Example of fair value
Buildings	Market-based evidence of fair value determined by professionally qualified valuer
Plant and equipment	Market-based evidence of fair value
Specialised items of PPE that are rarely sold	Fair value based on replacement cost as there is no market-based evidence

Lily Soaps Ltd has one tangible fixed asset, which is the equipment that was bought on 1 January 2015 at a cost of £13,000. Lily needs a method that will measure the proportion of the benefits that have been used up during the accounting period in order to make an allowance for depreciation on equipment. She estimates that the equipment has four years of useful life before technological advances mean it will become redundant. Nevertheless, at the end of four years she thinks the business will be able to sell it in the second-hand market for £1,000.

The accountant has suggested that the company uses the *straight-line method* of depreciation, which spreads the cost (or revalued amount) evenly over the life of the asset. It is calculated using the following formula:

$$\frac{\text{Cost} - \text{Residual value}}{\text{Useful life}}$$

Inserting the figures into the formula:

Working 2

$$\text{Depreciation on equipment} = \frac{£13,000 - £1,000}{4 \text{ years}} = £3,000$$

Lily can now add an allowance for depreciation on equipment of £3,000 to the other administrative expenses listed in the trial balance at 31 December 2015. We know that the cost of the asset was £13,000 and the equipment was bought on the first day of the accounting period (which for convenience we will call Year 0). At the end of the first year (Year 1), this figure will be reduced by the annual depreciation charge made in the statement of comprehensive income. This means that the cost of £13,000 will reduce by £3,000 each year for four years, and at the end of this time there will be a residual value of £1,000.

4.6   BAD DEBTS AND DOUBTFUL RECEIVABLES

A *bad debt* is one that is deemed to be irrecoverable. This may be because customers have died without leaving enough money to pay for their debts, become bankrupt or moved away without trace. This is an expense the business has to bear. It is written off as a charge against profit or against an existing allowance for doubtful receivables in the statement of comprehensive income. Fortunately, Lily Soaps Ltd has not had any bad debts, but Lily has been giving customers two months' credit and so far she has included all credit sales when calculating the total revenue for the year. Her accountant advises her that she should be prudent and make some provision for the possibility that some customers may not pay by making an *allowance for doubtful receivables*.

> **Definitions**
> A bad debt is an amount owed to the entity that is considered to be irrecoverable. It is written off as a charge against profit or against an existing allowance for doubtful receivables.
>
> An allowance for doubtful receivables is an amount charged against profit and deducted from receivables to allow for the estimated non-recovery of a proportion of debts.

The allowance for doubtful receivables can be based on specific debts where there is documentary evidence to suggest that the debts will not be paid. Another method that is used in some jurisdictions is based on the general assumption that a certain percentage of receivables are doubtful. However, it is not acceptable to the tax authorities in the UK.

> **Activity**
> The trial balance for Lily Soaps Ltd at 31 December 2015 shows that revenue for the year was £173,200 which comprised cash sales of £63,750 and credit sales of £109,450. Trade receivables were £27,500. If Lily Soaps Ltd makes an allowance for doubtful receivables of 10%, which of the following figures is the correct amount?
>
> (a) £17,320
> (b) £6,375
> (c) £10,945
> (d) £2,750

The first amount is 10% of the total sales revenue, but this includes cash sales so this answer is wrong because they have been paid for. The figure of £6,375 is 10% of the cash sales, but this is wrong for the same reason. The amount of £10,945 is 10% of credit sales for the year, but this too is wrong because the business has received payments from some of these customers. You need to calculate 10% of the trade receivables of £27,500:

> Working 3
> Doubtful receivables = £27,500 × 10% = £2,750

Lily must now include an allowance for doubtful receivables amounting to £2,750 as an additional expense to those listed in the trial balance. Consistency enhances comparability, so she will use the same method every year unless there is good reason to change it. Supposing the company has trade receivables of £25,000 in Year 2 because Lily has improved the credit control system, and she continues to make a 10% allowance for doubtful receivables. The calculation will be:

$$£25,000 × 10% = £2,500$$

This represents a decrease of £250 on Year 1 (£2,500 in Year 2 minus £2,750 in Year 1). Therefore, the allowance for doubtful receivables in Year 2 will decrease expenses by £250. If trade receivables in Year 3 are £26,000, the allowance for doubtful receivables will be:

$$£26,000 × 10% = £2,600$$

This is an increase of £100 on Year 2 (£2,600 in Year 3 minus £2,500 in Year 2). Therefore, the allowance for doubtful receivables in Year 3 will increase expenses by £100.

4.7   FINALISING THE STATEMENT OF COMPREHENSIVE INCOME

Lily's accountant has explained that classifying the company's expenses by function rather than by nature would reduce disclosure of information about costs that may be useful to competitors. Classifying expenses by function means that, instead of listing the individual expenses, they are grouped into three categories: distribution costs, administrative expenses and finance costs. The guiding principle is that the classification should result in information that is relevant and reliable. We now have all the information we need to finalise the statement of comprehensive income for Lily Soaps Ltd for the year ended 31 December 2015. Overleaf are the trial balance and the notes that represent the post trial balance adjustments we have just examined. In practice, all the post trial balance adjustments would be entered in the ledger accounts and a revised trial balance would be generated. However, we have shown the post trial balance information as notes because this is the way you are likely to encounter it in your assessments.

Lily Soaps Ltd
Trial balance at 31 December 2015

	Debit	Credit
	£	£
Revenue		173,200
Purchases	113,400	
Equipment (at cost)	13,000	
Trade receivables	27,500	
Trade payables		15,000
Cash	26,100	
Salaries	14,500	
Rent	6,000	
Telephone and Internet	1,960	
Printing, postage and stationery	1,100	
Advertising	600	
Interest on loan	540	
Loan		6,500
Share capital at 1 January 2015		10,000
	204,700	204,700

Additional information available at 31 December 2015:

- Closing inventory is valued at £750.
- Rent, printing, postage and stationery, and salaries are allocated 50% to distribution costs and 50% to administrative expenses.
- Advertising is classified as a distribution expense and telephone and Internet are classified as an administrative expense.
- There are accrued expenses of £100 for advertising and £200 for telephone and Internet.
- Printing, postage and stationery include a prepayment of £100.
- The equipment is expected to have a useful life of four years, and an estimated residual value of £1,000. Depreciation on equipment will be charged 50% to distribution costs and 50% to administrative expenses.
- An allowance for doubtful receivables will be based on 10% of trade receivables. This allowance will be charged 100% to administrative expenses.
- Income tax to be paid by 31 January 2016 will be £8,970.
- Lily is the sole shareholder of the company and shareholders normally expect to receive a return from their investment. However, Lily decides to leave all profits in the company to help it grow, rather than take some out in the form of a dividend.

> **Activity**
> Using the relevant items listed in the trial balance and all the additional information provided for the post trial balance adjustments, prepare a statement of comprehensive income for Lily Soaps Ltd for the year ended 31 December 2015.

You will find it useful to start by drawing together all the workings we made earlier in connection with the post trial balance adjustments at 31 December 2015. Then check your figures against Working 4 that classifies these expenses by function rather than by nature.

Working 4	Amount	Distribution costs	Administrative expenses	Finance costs
	£	£	£	£
Rent	6,000	3,000	3,000	
Advertising (600 + 100)	700	700		
Telephone and Internet (1,960 + 200)	2,160		2,160	
Printing, postage and stationery (1,100 − 100)	1,000	500	500	
Interest paid on loan	540			540
Salaries	14,500	7,250	7,250	
Depreciation on equipment (W2)	3,000	1,500	1,500	
Doubtful receivables (W3)	2,750		2,750	
Total	30,650	12,950	17,160	540

Your completed financial statement should look like this.

Lily Soaps Ltd **Statement of comprehensive income for the year ended 31 December 2015**	
	£
Revenue	173,200
Cost of sales (W1)	(112,650)
Gross profit	60,550
Distribution costs (W2, W3, W4)	(12,950)
Administrative expenses (W2, W3, W4)	(17,160)
Operating profit	30,440

(Continued)

Finance costs (W4)	(540)
Profit before tax	29,900
Income tax expense	(8,970)
Profit for the period	20,930

This is a fairly simple statement of comprehensive income because Lily Soaps Ltd does not have any items to show under Other comprehensive income. As it is the company's first year of trading, it is not possible to provide comparative figures for the previous year. You will find it useful to learn the following general layout for the statement of comprehensive income.

Name of entity **Statement of comprehensive income for the year ended (date)**	This year	Last year
	£	£
Revenue	X	X
Cost of sales	(X)	(X)
Gross profit	X	X
Other income	X	X
Distribution costs	(X)	(X)
Administrative expenses	(X)	(X)
Other expenses	(X)	(X)
Operating profit	X	X
Finance costs	(X)	(X)
Profit before tax	X	X
Income tax expense	(X)	(X)
Profit for the period	X	X
Other comprehensive income		
Gains on property revaluation	X	X
Available for sale financial assets	X	X
Income tax relating to other comprehensive income	(X)	(X)
Total comprehensive income for the period	X	X

Common mistakes made when preparing a statement of comprehensive income are:

- Not showing the name of the business.
- Not stating the period covered by the financial statement.
- Forgetting to include the currency symbol.
- Confusing opening inventory with closing inventory.
- Not making all the post trial balance adjustments.
- Forgetting to show any workings.
- Forgetting that it is only the final figure that is double underlined.

4.8   KEY POINTS

The statement of comprehensive income is one of the four financial statements that are prepared by reporting entities at the end of the accounting period. Its purpose is to measure the financial performance of the business over the accounting period, which is usually one year. This chapter has focused on how to prepare a statement of comprehensive income for a simple trading business with post trial balance adjustments.

REVISION QUESTIONS

1. Describe the general purpose of the statement of comprehensive income. In addition, explain the terms *income* and *expenses* as defined by the *Conceptual Framework for Financial Reporting* (IASB, 2010).
2. Explain the accrual basis of accounting by defining the principles involved. Illustrate your answer by taking the example of the cost of sales adjustment in the statement of comprehensive income.
3. Anika Inman set up a company called Uptown Ltd on 1 January 2015. Her brother helps with the bookkeeping and managing the inventory. At the end of the first year of trading, he generates the trial balance overleaf from the accounting records.

Uptown Ltd Trial balance at 31 December 2015		
	Debit	Credit
	£	£
Revenue		66,500
Purchases	20,000	
Fixtures and fittings (at cost)	20,000	
Trade receivables	2,000	
Trade payables		8,400
Cash	14,500	
Bank interest received		100
Rent and rates	24,000	
Salaries	21,500	
Insurance	2,000	
Lighting and heating	500	
Telephone and Internet	400	
Advertising	100	
Share capital at 1 January 2015		30,000
	105,000	105,000

Additional information at 31 December 2015:

- Inventory is valued at £8,000.
- Estimated current tax payable is £2,000.
- The company classifies expenses by nature.

Required

Use the relevant figures in the above information to prepare a draft statement of comprehensive income for Uptown Ltd for the year ended 31 December 2015. Show all your workings.

4. On 1 July 2014 Sergio Bari started a business called MiGame Ltd. The trial balance for the first year is shown below.

MiGame Ltd Trial balance at 30 June 2015	Debit	Credit
	£	£
Revenue		75,200
Purchases	12,160	
Plant and equipment at cost	25,000	
Trade receivables	1,200	
Trade payables		1,600
Cash	3,260	
Other income		1,200
Salaries	24,000	
Rent and rates	18,000	
Insurance	7,200	
Advertising	860	
Lighting and heating	620	
Telephone and Internet	450	
General expenses	250	
Share capital at 1 July 2014		15,000
	93,000	93,000

Additional information at 30 June 2015:

- Inventory is valued at £890.
- Advertising paid in advance is £260.
- Accrued expenses are lighting and heating £540, telephone and Internet £290 and general expenses £160.
- Estimated current tax payable is £1,200.

Required

(a) Using a spreadsheet, prepare a draft statement of comprehensive income for MiGame Ltd for the year ended 30 June 2015, classifying expenses by nature.

(b) After taking advice from his accountant, Sergio decides to depreciate equipment using the straight-line method over five years, with no residual value. He also decides to make an allowance for doubtful receivables and has decided to base it on 10% of opening trade receivables. Make these adjustments to your spreadsheet and generate a revised statement of comprehensive income for MiGame Ltd, classifying expenses by nature.

(c) The accountant's final suggestion is that Sergio should reclassify the expenses by function: 50% to distribution costs and 50% to administrative expenses, with the exception of advertising which should be allocated 100% to distribution costs and the allowance for doubtful receivables which should be allocated 100% to administrative expenses. Make these changes to your spreadsheet and generate a revised statement of comprehensive income for MiGame Ltd, classifying the expenses by function.

5. Beauty Plus Ltd started trading on 1 July 2014. At the end of the second year of trading, the bookkeeper provides the following trial balance from the accounting system.

Beauty Plus Ltd Trial balance at 30 June 2016		
	Debit	Credit
	£	£
Revenue		104,900
Purchases	39,700	
Inventory at 1 July 2015	10,000	
Equipment at cost	20,000	
Trade receivables	6,000	
Trade payables		8,000
Cash and cash equivalents	15,300	
Interest received		100
Salaries	30,000	

(Continued)

Rent and rates	15,000	
Insurance	3,000	
Lighting and heating	1,500	
Telephone and Internet	2,000	
Advertising	500	
Allowances at 1 July 2015:		
Depreciation on plant and equipment		4,000
Doubtful receivables		1,000
Share capital at 1 July 2015		20,000
Retained profit at 1 July 2015		5,000
	143,000	143,000

Additional information at 30 June 2016:

- Inventory is valued at £12,000.
- Equipment has a useful life of five years and no residual value. It is depreciated using the straight-line method.
- The company makes an allowance for doubtful receivables based on 10% of opening trade receivables.
- Estimated current tax liability is £4,500.
- The company classifies expenses by nature.

Required
Use the relevant figures in the above information to prepare a statement of comprehensive income for Beauty Plus Ltd for the year ended 30 June 2016. Show all your workings.

5

STATEMENT OF FINANCIAL POSITION

5.1 OBJECTIVES

Under IAS 1, *Presentation of Financial Statements* (IASB, 2011a), a complete set of financial statements includes a statement of financial position. After studying this chapter, you should be able to:
- Explain the purpose of the statement of financial position.
- Differentiate between non-current assets and current assets.
- Differentiate between non-current liabilities and current liabilities.
- Calculate depreciation using the reducing balance method.
- Prepare a statement of financial position.

5.2 PURPOSE OF THE STATEMENT OF FINANCIAL POSITION

Users of general purpose financial statements (see Chapter 3) have a common interest in information about the effects of transactions and other events that change a reporting entity's economic resources and claims. You know from Chapter 4 that this is shown in the *statement of comprehensive income*. However, users also need information about the entity's economic resources and the claims against the reporting entity and this information is shown in the *statement of financial position*. The elements that relate to the measurement of financial position are *assets*, *liabilities* and *equity*, which we defined in Chapter 2. *Assets* are what the business owns, such as premises, machinery, vehicles, equipment, inventory and cash. *Liabilities* are what the business owes to others apart from the owner, such as money owed to lenders and suppliers. What remains once the liabilities are subtracted from the assets is known as *equity*. Equity represents the owners' interest in the business and can be divided into the capital invested in the business by the owner(s) and retained earnings (profits left in the business to help it grow). The statement of financial position reflects the following accounting equation:

$$\text{Assets} = \text{Equity} + \text{Liabilities}$$

The point about any equation is that it balances: the total of the values on each side of the equation are equal. In this case, the equation states that the assets of the entity are always equal to the claims against them (the equity and other liabilities).

The purpose of the *statement of financial position* is to summarise the assets, equity and liabilities of the business on the last day of the accounting period for which the statement of comprehensive income was prepared. Because it looks at what the business owns and owes at one particular point in time, it is sometimes referred to as a 'financial snapshot'.

5.3   DRAFT STATEMENT OF FINANCIAL POSITION

The statement of financial position is presented in two parts. Although IAS 1, *Presentation of Financial Statements* (IASB, 2011a) and the *IFRS for SMEs* (IASB, 2009b) suggest how the statement of financial position should be presented, they do not prescribe the format of the statement or the order in which the items should be shown. The format we are going to illustrate presents the assets in the first part of the statement and the equity and liabilities in the second part, which reflects the accounting equation. An entity must normally present a classified statement of financial position.

Assets are separated into two groups:

- *Non-current assets* are assets that are intended for continuing use in the business. You may find it helpful to think of them as the long-term assets of the business. Non-current assets are subdivided into *tangible* non-current assets and *intangible* non-current assets. Tangible assets are non-monetary assets with physical substance such as property, plant and equipment, and intangible assets are identifiable non-monetary assets without physical substance, such as brands, patents, copyrights and licences. Other non-current assets include long-term investments.
- *Current assets* are not intended for continuing use in the business. You may find it helpful to think of them as the short-term assets of the business. In a business that trades or manufactures goods, current assets will be constantly changing from cash to inventory to trade receivables, to cash and possibly to short-term investments. Trade receivables are amounts owed by customers who have received goods or services on credit and have not yet paid.

Equity is separated into three groups:

- *Share capital* is the finance received by the company from its owner(s) in exchange for shares.
- *Retained earnings* are reserves of profits that are retained in the business to help it grow.
- *Other reserves* include funds arising from the issue of share capital at more than its nominal value.

Liabilities are separated into two groups:

- *Non-current liabilities* are amounts that are due to be paid to lenders and creditors more than one year after the date of the statement of financial position. You may find it helpful to think of them as long-term liabilities. Examples include long-term finance lease obligations, borrowings and employee benefit liabilities such as pensions.
- *Current liabilities* are amounts due to be paid to lenders and creditors within one year of the date of the statement of financial position. You may find it helpful to think of them as short-term liabilities. Examples include trade and other payables, dividends payable, current tax liability and short-term provisions, borrowings and finance lease liabilities. Trade payables are amounts due to suppliers who have supplied goods or services on credit and have not yet been paid.

The classification of assets, equity and liabilities in the statement of financial position is summarised in Figure 5.1.

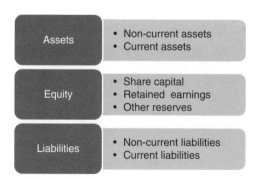

Figure 5.1 Classifying assets, equity and liabilities

You need to remember that accountants distinguish between revenue expenditure and capital expenditure:

- *Revenue expenditure* is the collective term for the costs and expenses that are written off in the statement of comprehensive income for the accounting period to which they relate.
- *Capital expenditure* is the collective term for the cost of non-current assets that are capitalised in the statement of financial position.

Example

You will remember that Lily Zhang started Lily Soaps Ltd on 1 January 2015. On that day she opened a business bank account with her savings of £10,000 and took out a loan of £6,500, which was also put into the business bank account. Using the company credit card, she then bought office equipment for £13,000 which would not need to be paid for until February.

It is important to remember that financial accounting and reporting is guided by the *business entity concept* (see Chapter 3). Therefore, Lily Soaps Ltd is considered to exist separately from its owner, Lily Zhang. This separation is crucial because the statement of financial position shows the financial position of the business and not that of its owner. On 1 January 2015 the draft statement of financial position for Lily Soaps Ltd looked like this.

Lily Soaps Ltd Draft statement of financial position at 1 January 2015	
	£
ASSETS	
Non-current assets	
Equipment (at cost)	13,000
Current assets	
Cash and cash equivalents	16,500
Total assets	29,500
EQUITY AND LIABILITIES	
Equity	
Share capital	(10,000)
Non-current liabilities	
Loan	(6,500)

(Continued)

Current liabilities	
Trade and other payables	(13,000)
Total equity and liabilities	**(29,500)**

As you can see, the name of the business and the date at which the statement of financial position has been prepared is given at the top of the statement. The assets on that date are listed in the first part of the statement and the equity and liabilities in the second part. Moreover, the total assets are equal to the total equity and liabilities. The order in which the assets are shown is based on liquidity, starting with those that would take the longest to turn into cash and ending with the most liquid. The order in which the liabilities are shown is based on immediacy, starting with long-term liabilities and ending with those that must be paid the soonest.

A statement of financial position can be prepared at any moment in time, so we will move forward to 2 January, by which time Lily has started trading by buying 100 boxes of soap at £15 each, which the business will not need to pay for until February.

Lily Soaps Ltd **Draft statement of financial position at 2 January 2015**	
	£
ASSETS	
Non-current assets	
Equipment (at cost)	13,000
Current assets	
Inventory	1,500
Cash and cash equivalents	16,500
	18,000
Total assets	**31,000**
EQUITY AND LIABILITIES	
Equity	
Share capital	(10,000)
Non-current liabilities	
Loan	(6,500)

(Continued)

Current liabilities	
Trade and other payables	(14,500)
Total equity and liabilities	**(31,000)**

As you can see, although the figures have changed, the statement of financial position still balances. The business has £31,000 in assets, which have been financed by a combination of Lily's capital and creditors. Current liabilities are £13,000 owing on the company credit card for the equipment and £1,500 owed to the supplier for the soap bought in January, giving a total of £14,500. Credit cards and credit agreed with suppliers are useful sources of interest-free credit as long as the debt is paid off within the agreed period.

We will now move on to the end of the first six months and prepare a draft statement of financial position at 30 June 2015. The following information is available:

- On 1 January, Lily Soaps Ltd bought office equipment for £13,000 which was paid for in full in February. The equipment is for long-term use in the business.
- The value of closing inventory at 30 June was £2,250 (150 boxes of soap at £15).
- Since the company allows credit customers two months to pay, customers buying in May and June have not yet paid. Therefore trade receivables are £16,700 (total credit sales for the period of £40,700 minus £24,000 cash received from credit sales).
- The company had a cash surplus of £500 at 30 June.
- Lily has invested £10,000 capital in the business and the company is also financed by a medium-term bank loan of £6,500.
- We know from the draft statement of comprehensive income for the six months ending 30 June 2015 (see Chapter 4) that the profit for the period was £4,865.
- Lily has not taken any of the profit as dividends.
- Trade suppliers give one month's credit, which means that inventory purchased in June has not yet been paid for. Therefore, trade payables are £9,000 (total purchases of £45,900 minus £36,900 cash paid to suppliers).
- The estimated current tax liability is £2,085.

Activity
Using the pro forma overleaf, prepare a draft statement of financial position for Lily Soaps Ltd at 30 June 2015.

Lily Soaps Ltd	
Draft statement of financial position at 30 June 2015	
	£
ASSETS	
Non-current assets	
Equipment (at cost)	_____
Current assets	
Inventory	
Trade and other receivables	
Cash and cash equivalents	_____
Total assets	_____
EQUITY AND LIABILITIES	
Equity	
Share capital	
Retained earnings	_____
Non-current liabilities	_____
Loan	
Current liabilities	
Trade and other payables	_____
Current tax liability	_____
Total equity and liabilities	_____

Your completed statement of financial position should look like this:

Lily Soaps Ltd	
Draft statement of financial position at 30 June 2015	
	£
ASSETS	
Non-current assets	
Equipment (at cost)	13,000
Current assets	
Inventory	2,250
Trade and other receivables	16,700
Cash and cash equivalents	500
	19,450
Total assets	**32,450**

(Continued)

EQUITY AND LIABILITIES	
Equity	
Share capital	(10,000)
Retained earnings	(4,865)
	(14,865)
Non-current liabilities	
Loan	(6,500)
Current liabilities	
Trade and other payables	(9,000)
Current tax liability	(2,085)
	(17,585)
Total equity and liabilities	(32,450)

We will now look at how the statement of financial position is prepared from a trial balance with *post trial balance adjustments*. Here is the trial balance at 31 December 2015, which is the end of the first year of trading for Lily Soaps Ltd.

Lily Soaps Ltd Trial balance at 31 December 2015		
	Debit	Credit
	£	£
Revenue		173,200
Purchases	113,400	
Equipment (at cost)	13,000	
Trade receivables	27,500	
Trade payables		15,000
Cash and cash equivalents	26,100	
Salaries	14,500	
Rent	6,000	
Telephone and Internet	1,960	
Postage and packing	1,100	
Advertising	600	
Interest on loan	540	
Loan		6,500
Share capital at 1 January 2015		10,000
	204,700	204,700

5.4   INVENTORY, ACCRUALS AND PREPAYMENTS

Inventory

As explained in the previous chapter, IAS 2, *Inventories* (IASB, 2003) and the *IFRS for SMEs* (IASB, 2009b) require inventory to be valued at the lower of cost or net realisable value (NRV). Lily carried out a stocktaking exercise on 31 December 2015 and found that Lily Soaps Ltd had 50 boxes of soap in stock which had cost £15 each. Therefore the value of closing inventory is £15 × 50 = £750. In Chapter 4 you made an adjustment in the statement of comprehensive income for the first year of trading ending 31 December 2015, by deducting £750 from the cost of purchases. Since inventory is one of the assets of the business that it hopes to sell in the next accounting period, you need to make a corresponding adjustment in the statement of financial position by showing £750 of closing inventory under current assets.

Accruals

An *accrual* is an estimate of a liability that is not supported by an invoice or a request for payment at the time when the accounts are prepared. Lily Soaps Ltd has two accrued expenses at 31 December 2015:

- The trial balance shows telephone and Internet expenses were £1,960, but there is an accrual of £200. This means that the expense shown in the statement of comprehensive income is £1,960 + £200 = £2,160.
- The trial balance shows that advertising expenses were £3,000, but there is an accrual of £100. Therefore, the expense shown in the statement of comprehensive income is £3,000 + £100 = £3,100.

You now need to make a corresponding adjustment in the statement of financial position by adding together the accruals (£200 + £100 = £300) and including this aggregated amount in the calculation of trade and other payables. Trade and other payables are shown under current liabilities because they will be paid during the next accounting period.

Prepayments

A *prepayment* is a payment made for goods or services before they are received. The amount that belongs to the next accounting period needs to be deducted from the trial balance figure for that expense. Lily Soaps Ltd has one prepayment at 31 December 2015:

- The trial balance shows postage and packing expenses were £1,100 in the accounts, but there is a prepayment of £100. Therefore the expense shown in the statement of comprehensive income should be £1,100 – £100 = £1,000.

You now need to make a corresponding adjustment in the statement of financial position. The general rule is to include the aggregated prepaid amounts in the calculation of trade and other receivables which are shown under current assets.

5.5   DEPRECIATION OF PROPERTY, PLANT AND EQUIPMENT

In Chapter 4 we explained that under IAS 16, *Property, Plant and Equipment* (IASB, 2008) and the *IFRS for SMEs* (IASB, 2009b) all items of plant, property and equipment (PPE) with a finite life must be depreciated. *Depreciation* is the systematic allocation of the depreciable amount of an asset over its useful life and the *depreciable amount* is the cost of the asset, or other amount substituted for cost, less its residual value. Lily Soaps Ltd has one tangible non-current asset:

- Equipment was bought on 1 January at a cost of £13,000. The equipment has a residual value of £1,000 at the end of its useful life of four years. The accountant has advised Lily to use the *straight-line method* of depreciation which spreads the cost (or revalued amount) evenly over the life of the asset.

As explained in Chapter 4, the allowance for depreciation included in the administrative expenses in the statement of comprehensive income for the year ended 31 December 2015 is calculated as follows:

$$\frac{\text{Cost} - \text{Residual value}}{\text{Useful life}} = \frac{£13,000 - £1,000}{4 \text{ years}} = £3,000$$

Since part of the cost of the asset has been apportioned as an expense for the period, you now need to make an adjustment to the value of the asset in the statement of financial position. Instead of showing the asset at cost, as Lily did when preparing the draft statement of financial position, the accountant tells her that it will be shown at the *carrying amount* (sometimes referred to as the net book value or the written down value of the asset). This is the amount at which an asset is recognised after deducting any accumulated depreciation and accumulated impairment losses. The residual value and useful life must be reviewed annually. If an asset is revalued, the valuation is substituted for the carrying amount and this will result in a revaluation gain or loss. An impairment loss is a reduction in the recoverable amount of the asset due to obsolescence, damage or a fall in the market value of such assets.

The equipment was bought on 1 January and at the end of the first year the carrying amount is calculated as follows:

$$\text{Cost} - \text{Depreciation} = £13,000 - £3,000 = £10,000$$

The closing carrying amount at the end of one year becomes the opening carrying amount at the start of the next, and each year the opening carrying amount will be reduced by £3,000 until at the end of the fourth year only the residual value of £1,000 remains. The following table illustrates a convenient way of setting out your workings.

Year	Opening carrying amount	Allowance for depreciation	Closing carrying amount
	£	£	£
1	13,000	(3,000)	10,000
2	10,000	(3,000)	7,000
3	7,000	(3,000)	4,000
4	4,000	(3,000)	1,000

Lily's accountant tells her about a second method that can be used. It is known as the *diminishing balance method* of depreciation because the cost reduces over the life of the asset. The method involves applying a depreciation rate to the opening carrying amount each year. In the first year, the opening carrying amount is the cost of the asset and the formula is:

$$\text{Cost} \times \text{Depreciation rate (\%)}$$

In subsequent years the formula is:

$$\text{Opening carrying amount} \times \text{Depreciation rate (\%)}$$

The table opposite shows how the diminishing balance method would be applied to the equipment. As a very rough rule of thumb, the depreciation rate is nearly double that required for the straight-line method. Since the annual allowance for depreciation under the straight-line method was 25% (£3,000 ÷ £12,000), we will use a rate of 47.25% in this illustration of the diminishing balance method. The first step is to calculate the allowance for depreciation for the first year:

$$£13,000 \times 47.25\% = £6,143$$

We can now use this to work out the closing carrying amount at the end of Year 1 (£6,858), which becomes the opening carrying amount for Year 2. The depreciation rate of 47.25% is then applied to find the depreciation charge for Year 2 (£6,858 × 47.25% = £3,240). This is then deducted from the opening carrying amount to arrive at the closing carrying amount. This continues until the end of Year 4, when the following table shows that we are left with the residual value of just over £1,000.

Year	Opening carrying amount	Depreciation 47.25%	Closing carrying amount
	£	£	£
1	13,000	(6,143)	6,858
2	6,858	(3,240)	3,617
3	3,617	(1,709)	1,908
4	1,908	(902)	1,007

Lily's accountant also mentions that methods based on usage, such as the units of production method, are also permitted. These would be relevant to businesses in the manufacturing sector. The depreciation method chosen should reflect the pattern in which the asset's economic benefits are consumed by the entity. If the pattern by which the entity expects to consume an asset's future economic benefits has changed significantly since the last annual reporting date, management must review the present depreciation method. If the differences are expected to continue, the method should be changed to reflect the new pattern.

The straight-line method is widely used as it is simple and easy to use and apportions the cost of the asset evenly over its useful life to the business. If the pattern in which the economic benefits are consumed is uncertain, the straight-line method is usually adopted. Although the diminishing balance method is more complex, the lower depreciation charge in later years helps to offset higher maintenance costs that are likely when assets such as plant, machinery and vehicles age. Thus the overall cost of such assets is spread evenly. To aid comparison, the same depreciation method is used for all assets that are classified as belonging to the same group and it is applied consistently from one period to the next.

5.6   BAD DEBTS AND DOUBTFUL RECEIVABLES

A *bad debt* is an amount owed by customers that is considered to be irrecoverable and it must be written off as a charge against profit or against an existing allowance for doubtful receivables in the statement of comprehensive income. As mentioned in the previous chapter, Lily Soaps Ltd did not have any bad debts during the first year of trading. Lily's accountant has advised her to make an *allowance for doubtful receivables* to allow for the estimated non-recovery of receivables. Lily has decided to base the allowance on 10% of trade receivables: £27,500 × 10% = £2,750. Therefore, this is the amount that was included in the distribution costs in the statement of comprehensive income and needs to be deducted from the trade receivables figure shown in the trial balance before using it in the statement of financial position.

Lily's accountant tells her about an alternative method based on the age of the debt. The following table shows an age analysis of the company's trade receivables. Most debts are two months old or less because the business gives customers two months to pay. However, some debts are more than three months old, which means some customers are taking much longer than the agreed two months. If Lily does not improve her credit control, there is a risk that some customers will not pay and this is reflected in the higher percentages the accountant has applied to older debts when calculating the allowance for doubtful receivables.

Age of debt (months)	Trade receivables	Estimated bad receivables	Allowance for doubtful receivables
	£		£
1	12,500	1%	125
2	10,500	10%	1,050
3	3,000	50%	1,500
4 or more	1,500	75%	1,125
Total	27,500		3,800

For financial reporting purposes, the entity should choose the method that gives the most realistic allowance and then use it consistently to aid comparability.

5.7   FINALISING STATEMENT OF FINANCIAL POSITION

We now have all the information we need to prepare the statement of comprehensive income for Lily Soaps Ltd for the year ended 31 December 2015 and the statement of financial position at that date. Here is the trial balance and the notes that represent the post trial balance adjustments. In practice, all the post trial balance adjustments would be entered in the ledger accounts and a revised trial balance would be generated. However, we have shown the post trial balance information as notes, as this is the way you are likely to encounter it in your assessments.

Lily Soaps Ltd **Trial balance at 31 December 2015**	Debit	Credit
	£	£
Revenue		173,200
Purchases	113,400	
Equipment (at cost)	13,000	
Trade receivables	27,500	
Trade payables		15,000
Cash and cash equivalents	26,100	
Salaries	14,500	
Rent	6,000	
Telephone and Internet	1,960	
Printing, postage and stationery	1,100	
Advertising	600	
Interest on loan	540	
Loan		6,500
Share capital at 1 January 2015		10,000
	204,700	204,700

Additional information available at 31 December 2015:

- Closing inventory is valued at £750.
- Rent, printing, postage and stationery, and salaries are allocated 50% to distribution costs and 50% to administrative expenses.
- Advertising is classified as a distribution expense.
- Telephone and Internet are classified as administrative expenses.
- There are accruals of £100 for advertising and £200 for telephone and Internet.
- Printing, postage and packaging include a prepayment of £100.
- The equipment is expected to have a useful life of four years, and an estimated residual value of £1,000. Depreciation on equipment will be charged 50% to distribution costs and 50% to administrative expenses.
- An allowance for doubtful receivables will be made based on 10% of trade receivables and will be charged 100% to distribution costs.
- The estimated current tax liability is £8,970.
- Lily has decided to leave all profits in the company to help it grow, rather than take some for herself in the form of a dividend.

> **Activity**
> Prepare a statement of comprehensive income for Lily Soaps Ltd for the year ended 31 December 2015 and a statement of financial position at 31 December 2015 using all the items listed in the trial balance and taking account of every item of additional information provided for the post trial balance adjustments.

You will find it helpful to tick each item as you use it. When you have finished, all the items in the trial balance will have one tick because they are either shown in the statement of comprehensive income or the statement of financial position. On the other hand, every item in the notes represents a post trial balance adjustment so it will have two ticks: one for when you show the adjustment in the statement of comprehensive income and the other for when you show the adjustment in the statement of financial position.

Start by drawing together all the calculations we made in connection with the post trial balance adjustments at 31 December 2015:

Working 1	£
Purchases	113,400
Closing inventory	(750)
Cost of sales	112,650

Put one tick against the information about closing inventory when you use it to calculate cost of sales in the statement of comprehensive income, and another when you include it under current assets in the statement of financial position.

Working 2

$$\text{Depreciation on equipment} = \frac{£13,000 - £1,000}{4 \text{ years}} = £3,000$$

$$\text{Closing carrying amount} = £13,000 - £3,000 = £10,000$$

Put one tick against the information about the allowance for depreciation on equipment when you use it to calculate distribution costs and administrative expenses in the statement of comprehensive income, and another when you show the carrying amount of equipment under non-current assets in the statement of financial position.

Working 3

Allowance for doubtful receivables = £27,500 × 10% = £2,750

Put one tick against the information about the allowance for doubtful receivables when you use it to calculate distribution costs and administrative expenses in the statement of comprehensive income, and another when you include it the calculation of trade and other receivables under current assets in the statement of financial position.

Working 4	Amount	Distribution costs	Administrative expenses	Finance costs
	£	£	£	£
Rent	6,000	3,000	3,000	
Advertising (600 + 100)	700	700		
Telephone and Internet (1,960 + 200)	2,160		2,160	
Printing, postage and stationery (1,100 − 100)	1,000	500	500	
Interest paid on loan	540			540
Salaries	14,500	7,250	7,250	
Depreciation (W2)		3,000	1,500	1,500
Doubtful receivables (W3)	2,750		2,750	
Total	30,650	12,950	17,160	540

Working 5	£
Trade receivables in trial balance	27,500
Doubtful receivables (10%)	(2,750)
Trade receivables	24,750
Prepayments	100
Trade and other receivables	24,850

Working 6	£
Trade payables in trial balance	15,000
Accruals	300
Trade and other payables	15,300

Your completed financial statements should look like this.

Lily Soaps Ltd
Statement of comprehensive income for the year ended 31 December 2015

	£
Revenue	173,200
Cost of sales (W1)	(112,650)
Gross profit	60,550
Distribution costs (W2, W3, W4)	(12,950)
Administrative expenses (W2, W3, W4)	(17,160)
Operating profit	30,440
Finance costs (W4)	(540)
Profit before tax	29,900
Income tax expense	(8,970)
Profit for the period	20,930

Lily Soaps Ltd
Statement of financial position at 31 December 2015

	£
ASSETS	
Non-current assets	
Equipment (W2)	10,000
Current assets	
Inventory	750
Trade and other receivables (W5)	24,850
Cash and cash equivalents	26,100
	51,700
Total assets	61,700
EQUITY AND LIABILITIES	
Equity	
Share capital	(10,000)
Retained earnings	(20,930)
	(30,930)

(Continued)

Non-current liabilities	
Loan	(6,500)
Current liabilities	
Trade and other payables (W6)	(15,300)
Current tax liability	(8,970)
	(30,770)
Total equity and liabilities	(61,700)

These are fairly simple financial statements and, because it is the company's first year of trading, it is not possible to provide comparative figures for the previous year. You will find it useful to learn the following more detailed layout for the statement of financial position, which is consistent with the minimum requirements of IAS 1.

Name of entity **Statement of financial position at (date)**	This year	Last year
	£	£
ASSETS		
Non-current assets		
Property, plant and equipment	X	X
Intangible assets	X	X
Investments	X	X
	X	X
Current assets		
Inventories	X	X
Trade and other receivables	X	X
Investments	X	X
Cash and cash equivalents	X	X
	X	X
Total assets	X	X

(Continued)

EQUITY AND LIABILITIES		
Equity		
Share capital	X	X
Retained earnings	X	X
Other reserves	X	X
	X	X
Non-current liabilities		
Finance lease liabilities	X	X
Borrowings	X	X
	X	X
Current liabilities		
Trade and other payables	X	X
Dividends payable	X	X
Current tax liability	X	X
Provisions	X	X
Borrowings	X	X
Finance lease liabilities	X	X
	X	X
Total equity and liabilities	X	X

Common mistakes students make when drawing up the statement of financial position are:

- Not showing the name of the business.
- Not stating the date at which the statement of financial position is prepared.
- Forgetting to include the currency symbol.
- Confusing opening inventory with closing inventory.
- Not making all the post trial balance adjustments.
- Forgetting to show any workings.
- Not classifying assets and liabilities correctly.
- Forgetting that it is only the two balancing figures that are underlined (total assets in the first part and total equity and liabilities in the second part).

5.8 KEY POINTS

The statement of comprehensive income and the statement of financial position are two of the four financial statements that are prepared by reporting entities at the end of the accounting period. The purpose of the statement of comprehensive income is to measure the financial performance of the business over the accounting period, which is usually one year. This financial statement gives users important information about all profits and gains made by the entity over the period. In this chapter we have explained that the purpose of the statement of financial position is to measure the financial position of the business on the last day of the accounting period for which the statement of comprehensive income has been prepared. This second financial statement gives users important information about the assets, equity and other liabilities of the business.

REVISION QUESTIONS

1. Describe the general purpose of the statement of financial position. In addition, explain the terms *asset, liability* and *equity* as defined by the *Conceptual Framework for Financial Reporting* (IASB, 2010).
2. Explain the going concern basis of accounting by defining the principles involved. Illustrate your answer by taking the example of the valuation of tangible assets in the statement of financial position.
3. Anika Inman set up a company called Uptown Ltd on 1 January 2015. Her brother helps with the bookkeeping and managing the inventory. At the end of the first year of trading, he generates the following trial balance from the accounting records.

Uptown Ltd Trial balance at 31 December 2015		
	Debit	Credit
	£	£
Revenue		66,500
Purchases	20,000	
Fixtures and fittings (at cost)	20,000	
Trade receivables	2,000	

(Continued)

Trade payables		8,400
Cash	14,500	
Bank interest received		100
Rent and rates	24,000	
Salaries	21,500	
Insurance	2,000	
Lighting and heating	500	
Telephone and Internet	400	
Advertising	100	
Share capital at 1 January 2015		30,000
	105,000	105,000

Additional information at 31 December 2015:

- Inventory is valued at £8,000.
- Estimated current tax payable is £2,000.
- The company classifies expenses by nature.

Required
Prepare a draft statement of comprehensive income for Uptown Ltd for the year ended 31 December 2015 and a draft statement of financial position at that date. Show all your workings.

4. On 1 July 2014 Sergio Bari opened a shop called MiGame Ltd. The trial balance for the first year is shown below.

MiGame Ltd		
Trial balance at 30 June 2015		
	Debit	Credit
	£	£
Revenue		75,200
Purchases	12,160	
Plant and equipment at cost	25,000	

(Continued)

Trade receivables	1,200	
Trade payables		1,600
Cash and cash equivalents	3,260	
Other income		1,200
Salaries	24,000	
Rent and rates	18,000	
Insurance	7,200	
Advertising	860	
Lighting and heating	620	
Telephone and Internet	450	
General expenses	250	
Share capital at 1 July 2014		15,000
	93,000	93,000

Additional information at 30 June 2015:

- Inventory is valued at £890.
- Advertising paid in advance is £260.
- Accrued expenses are lighting and heating £540, telephone and Internet £290 and general expenses £160.
- Estimated current tax payable is £1,200.

Required

(a) Using a spreadsheet, prepare a draft statement of comprehensive income for MiGame Ltd for the year ended 30 June 2015 classifying expenses by nature. In addition, prepare a draft statement of financial position at that date.

(b) After taking advice from his accountant, Sergio has decided to depreciate equipment using the straight-line method over five years, with no residual value. He has also decided to make an allowance for doubtful receivables and has decided to base it on 10% of opening trade receivables. Make these adjustments to your spreadsheet and prepare a statement of comprehensive income for MiGame Ltd, classifying expenses by nature. In addition, prepare a statement of financial position at that date.

5. Beauty Plus Ltd started trading on 1 July 2014. At the end of the second year of trading, the bookkeeper provides the following trial balance from the accounting system.

Beauty Plus Ltd Trial balance at 30 June 2016	Debit	Credit
	£	£
Revenue		104,900
Purchases	39,700	
Inventory at 1 July 2015	10,000	
Equipment at cost	20,000	
Trade receivables	6,000	
Trade payables		8,000
Cash and cash equivalents	15,300	
Interest received		100
Salaries	30,000	
Rent and rates	15,000	
Insurance	3,000	
Lighting and heating	1,500	
Telephone and Internet	2,000	
Advertising	500	
Allowances at 1 July 2015:		
Depreciation on plant and equipment		4,000
Doubtful receivables		1,000
Share capital at 1 July 2015		20,000
Retained profit at 1 July 2015		5,000
	143,000	143,000

Additional information at 30 June 2016:

- Inventory is valued at £12,000.
- Equipment has a useful life of five years and no residual value. It is depreciated using the straight-line method.
- The company makes an allowance for doubtful receivables based on 10% of opening trade receivables.
- Estimated current tax liability is £4,500.
- The company classifies expenses by nature.

Required

Use the relevant figures in the above information to prepare a statement of comprehensive income for Beauty Plus Ltd for the year ended 30 June 2016. In addition, prepare a statement of financial position at that date. Show all your workings.

6

STATEMENT OF CASH FLOWS

6.1 OBJECTIVES

Under IAS 1, *Presentation of Financial Statements* (IASB, 2011a), a complete set of financial statements includes a statement of cash flows. After studying this chapter, you should be able to:
- Explain the purpose of the statement of cash flows.
- Differentiate between cash and cash equivalents.
- Classify cash flows into operating, investing or financing activities.
- Prepare a statement of cash flows using the direct method.
- Prepare a statement of cash flows using the indirect method.

6.2 PURPOSE OF THE STATEMENT OF CASH FLOWS

From Chapters 4 and 5 you know that users of general purpose financial statements have a common interest in information about the entity's economic resources and the claims against the reporting entity. This information is shown in the *statement of financial position*. Users of financial statements also need information about the effects of transactions and other events that change a reporting entity's economic resources and claims; in other words, the performance of the business over the accounting period. This is shown in the *statement of comprehensive income*. We are now ready to consider users' needs for information on the changes in the entity's cash flows, which is shown in the *statement of cash flows*.

The accruals basis of accounting means that a business can make a profit over the accounting period and yet it may not have enough cash at the end of the period to continue as a going concern. This leads to the saying, 'revenue is vanity, profit is sanity, but cash is reality'. The figure for revenue in the statement of comprehensive income has limited use because it does not take account of the costs and expenses incurred by the business. The profit figure is more informative because it reflects the financial performance of the business, but profit is not always a useful representation of the entity's operations. This is due to a number of reasons such as the following:

- Revenue includes credit sales, but the business may not receive payment for some sales until the next accounting period. In addition, some of these customers may return their goods for a refund and others may never pay.
- The business usually has only a short credit period within which to pay for purchases of inventory, but the cost of inventory has no impact on profit until the goods are sold.
- If the business acquires tangible assets with a finite life, there may be an immediate outflow of cash, but only the annual allowance for depreciation is included as an operating expense.
- If the business repays a loan or distributes dividends to investors, there is an immediate outflow of cash, but this transaction has no effect on profit.

Users need a financial statement that will help them evaluate the cash generating ability of the business and its liquidity. Cash is essential to the survival of the business. It needs cash for the following main reasons:

- To pay employees.
- To pay creditors.
- To acquire or replace equipment.
- To repay loans.
- To distribute dividends to investors.

The purpose of the statement of cash flows is to provide historical information about changes in cash and cash equivalents resulting from the inflows and outflows of cash. Cash inflows are the cash receipts of the business and cash outflows are the cash payments made by the business. The difference between the inflows and outflows of cash is known as the net cash flow (a positive figure indicates a cash surplus and a negative figure indicates a cash deficit).

Definition
Cash inflows are the cash receipts of a business.
Cash outflows are the cash payments made by a business.
Net cash flow is the difference between the cash inflows and the cash outflows.

The statement of cash flows calculates the change in cash and cash equivalents based on the following equation:

Cash inflows − Cash outflows = Change in cash and cash equivalents

6.3   CASH AND CASH EQUIVALENTS

IAS 7, *Statement of Cash Flows* (IASB, 2012) requires all entities that comply with IFRS to prepare a statement of cash flows which should provide information about the historical changes in *cash and cash equivalents*. This term should be familiar because it is one of the items shown under current assets in the statement of financial position. IAS 7 distinguishes between them as follows:

- Cash is defined as cash on hand and demand deposits. Examples of cash on hand are money and cheques held in the business or money at the bank. Examples of demand deposits are money held on short-term deposit at a bank or other financial institution.
- Cash equivalents are defined as short-term, highly liquid investments that are readily convertible to known amounts of cash and which are subject to insignificant risk of changes in value. Examples of cash equivalents are treasury bills, short-term government bonds and money market holdings. Cash equivalents are held for the purpose of meeting short-term cash commitments rather than for investment or other purposes.

An investment qualifies as a cash equivalent if it is readily convertible to a known amount of cash and is subject to an insignificant risk of changes in value. Therefore, an investment normally qualifies as a cash equivalent when it has a short maturity of, say, three months or less from the date of acquisition. Equity investments are excluded from cash equivalents unless they are, in substance, cash equivalents (such as preference shares acquired within a short period of their maturity and with a specified redemption date).

Bank overdrafts are generally classified as borrowings, but IAS 7 notes that if a bank overdraft is repayable on demand and forms an integral part of an entity's cash management, it is included as a component of cash and cash equivalents. A characteristic of such a banking arrangement is that the bank balance often fluctuates from being positive to overdrawn.

> **Definition**
>
> Cash comprises cash on hand and demand deposits.
>
> Cash equivalents are short-term, highly liquid investments that are readily convertible to known amounts of cash and which are subject to an insignificant risk of changes in value.
>
> Source: IAS 7, para 7 (IASB, 2012)

6.4 CLASSIFICATION OF CASH FLOWS

IAS 7 requires the information in the statement of cash flows to be classified into cash flows from three different activities: *operating*, *investing* and *financing activities*. These terms should be familiar as you used them in the statement of comprehensive income to distinguish between operating expenses, investment costs and finance costs. We will now look at them in more detail.

Operating activities are defined as the principal revenue-producing activities of the entity that are not investing or financing activities. Examples include:

- Cash receipts from customers.
- Cash receipts from other revenue, such as royalties and commissions.
- Cash payments to suppliers.
- Cash payments to and on behalf of employees.
- Cash payments in respect of interest on loans for operating purposes.
- Cash payments of income tax and receipts from income tax refunds relating to operating activities.

These cash flows relate to transactions and events reported in the statement of comprehensive income. The net cash flow from operating activities is an important measure of an entity's ability to generate sufficient cash to replace assets, pay dividends and make new investments without having to use external sources of finance. This information can also be used to forecast future operating cash flows.

Investing activities are defined as the acquisition and disposal of long-term assets and other investments not included in cash equivalents. Examples include:

- Cash receipts from the sale of redundant non-current assets and intangible assets.
- Cash receipts from the sale of equity or debt instruments (such as shares or debentures) of other entities.

- Cash receipts from the repayment of advances and loans made to other parties.
- Cash payments to acquire property, plant and equipment and intangible assets.
- Cash payments to acquire equity and debt instruments (such as shares or debentures) of other entities.
- Cash payments in respect of advances and loans made to other parties.

Financing activities are defined as activities that result in changes in the size and composition of the contributed equity and borrowings of the entity. Examples include:

- Cash receipts from issuing shares.
- Cash receipts from issuing debentures and loans.
- Cash payments to owners to acquire or redeem the entity's shares.
- Cash repayments of amounts borrowed or amounts paid to reduce a liability under a finance lease.

Definition

Operating activities are the principal revenue generating activities of the entity and other activities that are not investing or financing activities.

Investing activities are the acquisition and disposal of long-term assets and other investments not included in cash equivalents.

Financing activities are activities that result in changes in the size and composition of the contributed equity and borrowings of the entity.

Source: IAS 7, para 6 (IASB, 2012)

Normally it is fairly easy to classify the cash flows into one of these three categories. You need to bear in mind that all businesses have operating activities, but some may not have investing and/or financing activities. You may also find that you need to identify the elements within a transaction so that you can classify each element appropriately. For example, if a mortgage repayment also includes interest, the interest element may be classified as an operating activity and the repayment element as a financing activity. Interest and dividends received and paid may be classified as operating, investing or financing cash flows, as appropriate. However, they must be classified consistently from period to period. Cash flows arising from taxes on income are normally classified as operating activities, unless specifically identified with financing or investing activities.

   Classifying the inflows and outflows of cash according to the operating, investing and financing activities of the business provides useful information, but in order to calculate the change in cash and equivalents, we need to aggregate the net cash flow (NCF) from each category. This is reflected in the expanded equation that underpins the statement of cash flows:

NCF from operating activities + NCF from investing activities + NCF from financing activities = Change in cash and cash equivalents

IAS 7 allows two methods for reporting the cash flows from operating activities: the *direct method* and the *indirect method*. Both methods result in the same figure for the net cash flows from operating activities; it is merely the presentation and method of calculation that differs. However, IAS 7 encourages the use of the direct method, as it supplies more relevant information and is more understandable to users. The presentation of the cash flows from investing and financing activities does not differ between the methods.

6.5 CASH FLOWS FROM OPERATING ACTIVITIES UNDER THE DIRECT METHOD

Under the *direct method*, each major class of gross cash receipts and gross cash payments from operating activities is shown separately and then aggregated to give the total cash generated from operating activities.

Example

You will remember that Lily Zhang started the company on 1 January 2015 when she invested £10,000 in the business. The financial statements of Lily Soaps Ltd from Chapters 4 and 5 are reproduced below. You will see that the statement of financial position includes the comparative position at 1 January 2015 when the company started trading. In future years, the statement of financial position for the previous year will provide the comparative position.

Lily Soaps Ltd Statement of comprehensive income for the year ended 31 December 2015	
	£
Revenue	173,200
Cost of sales	(112,650)

(Continued)

Gross profit	60,550
Distribution costs	(12,950)
Administrative expenses	(17,160)
Operating profit	30,440
Finance costs	(540)
Profit before tax	29,900
Income tax expense	(8,970)
Profit for the period	20,930

Lily Soaps Ltd
Statements of financial position at

	31 Dec 2015	1 Jan 2015
	£	£
ASSETS		
Non-current assets		
Equipment	10,000	–
Current assets		
Inventory	750	–
Trade and other receivables	24,850	–
Cash and cash equivalents	26,100	10,000
	51,700	10,000
Total assets	61,700	10,000
EQUITY AND LIABILITIES		
Equity		
Share capital	(10,000)	10,000
Retained earnings	(20,930)	–
	(30,930)	10,000

(Continued)

Non-current liabilities		
Loan	(6,500)	–
Current liabilities		
Trade and other payables	(15,300)	–
Current tax liability	(8,970)	–
	(30,770)	10,000
Total equity and liabilities	(61,700)	10,000

The following information is also available at 31 December 2015:

- Distribution costs included depreciation on equipment of £1,500.
- Administrative expenses included salaries of £14,500, depreciation on equipment of £1,500 and an allowance for doubtful receivables of £2,750.
- There were no non-current asset disposals during the year to 31 December 2015 and no dividends were paid.
- Trade receivables were £27,500 less £2,750 allowance for doubtful receivables, and other receivables were prepaid expenses of £100.
- Trade payables were £15,000 and other payables were accrued expenses of £300.

We will now use this information to illustrate the operating section of the statement of cash flows under the direct method. You will find it useful to learn the following layout:

Cash flows from operating activities	£
Cash receipts from customers	X
Cash paid to suppliers	(X)
Cash paid to employees	(X)
Cash paid for other operating expenses	(X)
Cash generated from operating activities	X
Interest paid	(X)
Income taxes paid	(X)
Net cash flow from operating activities	X

Step 1. Calculate the cash flows from cash receipts from customers by adjusting revenue for opening and closing trade receivables as shown in Working 1.

Working 1	£
Revenue	173,200
Opening trade receivables	–
Opening allowance for doubtful receivables	–
Closing trade receivables	(24,750)
Closing allowance for doubtful receivables	(2,750)
Cash receipts from customers	145,700

Step 2. Calculate the cash paid to suppliers. Cash paid for inventory is calculated by adjusting purchases for opening and closing trade payables. There also needs to be an adjustment for the net increase or decrease in other payables. In this case, the other payables are accrued expenses of £300 and prepaid expenses of £100, so the net increase is £200. Cash paid for distribution costs and administrative expenses require adjustments for non-cash expenses (in this case, depreciation and the allowance for doubtful receivables). Finally, cash paid for salaries is excluded because salaries are shown separately. Working 2 shows these calculations.

Working 2	£
Cost of sales	112,650
Opening inventory	(–)
Closing inventory	750
Purchases	113,400
Opening trade payables	–
Closing trade payables	(15,000)
Distribution costs	12,950
Administrative expenses	17,160
Increase in accrued expenses	(300)
Increase in prepaid expenses	100
Depreciation on equipment	(3,000)
Allowance for doubtful receivables	(2,750)
Salaries	(14,500)
Cash payments to suppliers	108,060

Step 3. Calculate the cash paid to employees. This is straightforward as Lily Soaps Ltd paid the salaries of £14,500 in cash and there are no associated accruals or prepayments.

Step 4. Add the figures from the first three steps to provide the subtotal of cash generated from operating activities. Then adjust for any interest paid in connection with operating activities (£540 in this case) and income tax payments, to arrive at the net cash flow from operating activities. Although Lily Soaps Ltd incurred an income tax expense of £8,970 during 2015, this was unpaid at the year end, so no adjustment is necessary.

Activity

Complete step 4 and prepare the operating section of the statement of cash flows under the direct method.

Check your answer against the following:

Cash flows from operating activities	£
Cash receipts from customers	145,700
Cash paid to suppliers	(108,060)
Cash paid to employees	(14,500)
Cash generated from operating activities	23,140
Interest paid	(540)
Income taxes paid	(–)
Net cash flow from operating activities	22,600

6.6 CASH FLOWS FROM OPERATING ACTIVITIES UNDER THE INDIRECT METHOD

Under the *indirect method*, the starting point is the profit before tax, which is then adjusted for the effects of the following transactions which are part of the operating activities of the business:

- Non-cash expenses, such as depreciation, impairment of goodwill and any change in the allowance for doubtful receivables.
- Non-cash income, such as gains on the sale of non-current assets and a decrease in the allowance for doubtful receivables.

- Changes in non-cash working capital items, such as inventory, trade receivables, prepaid expenses, trade payables and accrued expenses.
- Items of income or expense associated with investing or financing cash flows.

Example

We will now use the indirect method to prepare a statement of cash flows for Lily Soaps Ltd for the year ended 31 December 2015, using the figures given in the statement of comprehensive income, statement of financial position and the additional information provided. You will find it useful to learn the following layout for the operating section of the statement of cash flows under the indirect method:

Cash flows from operating activities	£
Profit before tax	X
Depreciation	X
Impairment of assets	X
Increase in inventory	(X)
Increase in trade receivables	(X)
Increase in prepaid expenses	(X)
Increase in trade payables	X
Increase in accrued expenses	X
Cash generated from operating activities	X
Interest paid	X
Income taxes paid	X
Net cash flow from operating activities	X

Step 1. Adjust the profit before tax for expenses and income that do not involve a flow of cash. The general rule is to add back non-cash expenses, such as depreciation, impairment of goodwill and an increase in the allowance for doubtful receivables. The figures for Lily Soaps Ltd are shown in Working 1. As this is the first year of trading, there is no adjustment for changes in the allowance for doubtful receivables.

Working 1	£
Profit before tax	29,900
Depreciation	3,000

Step 2. Adjust for income that does not involve a flow of cash. The general rule is to deduct any non-cash income, such as a gain on disposal of a non-current assets or a decrease in the allowance for doubtful receivables. Lily Soaps Ltd has no non-cash income this year, as you can see from Working 2, so we can move on to the next step.

Working 2	£
Profit before tax	29,900
Depreciation	3,000
Non-cash income	(–)

Step 3. Adjust for changes in changes in non-cash working capital items. The general rule is to deduct an increase in inventory, trade receivables or prepaid expenses because they require more cash to be paid to suppliers (inventory and prepaid expenses) or delay the receipt of cash from customers (trade receivables). By the same logic, you add an increase in trade payables or accrued expenses because they mean less cash is being paid to suppliers. These adjustments are shown in Working 3.

Working 3	£
Profit before tax	29,900
Depreciation	3,000
Increase in inventory	(750)
Increase in trade receivables	(24,750)
Increase in prepaid expenses	(100)
Increase in trade payables	15,000
Increase in accrued expenses	300

A useful guide to remembering whether you are going to add the item to the operating profit or deduct it is to consider whether it reflects a cash flow. If it does not, it is a non-cash item and you need to add it back into profit. If it does have an effect on cash, you need to decide whether the increase or decrease in the item results in an increase or decrease in cash. Table 6.1 summarises the main adjustments we have covered in the above three steps.

Step 4. Using the figures from the first three steps, provide the subtotal of cash generated from operations. Then adjust for any interest paid in connection with operating activities (£540 in this case) and income tax payments, to arrive at the net cash flow from operating activities. Although Lily Soaps Ltd incurred an income tax expense of £8,970 during 2015, this was unpaid at the year end, so no adjustment is necessary.

Table 6.1 Main adjustments to operating income and expenses under the indirect method

Adjustment	Reason
Add depreciation	Non-cash item
Add an increase in the allowance for doubtful receivables	Non-cash item
Deduct a decrease in the allowance for doubtful receivables	Non-cash item
Add a decrease in inventory	Increases cash
Deduct an increase in inventory	Reduces cash
Add a decrease in trade receivables	Increases cash
Deduct an increase in trade receivables	Reduces cash
Add an increase in trade payables	Increases cash
Deduct a decrease in trade payables	Reduces cash
Add an increase in accrued expenses	Increases cash
Deduct a decrease in accrued expenses	Reduces cash
Add a decrease in prepaid expenses	Increases cash
Deduct an increase in prepaid expenses	Reduces cash

Activity
Complete step 4 and prepare the operating section of the statement of cash flows under the indirect method.

You should have found this easy as it is similar to what you did when using the direct method. Check your answer against the following:

Cash flows from operating activities	£
Profit before tax	29,900
Depreciation	3,000
Increase in inventory	(750)
Increase in trade receivables	(24,750)
Increase in prepaid expenses	(100)

(Continued)

Increase in trade payables	15,000
Increase in accrued expenses	300
Cash generated from operating activities	23,140
Interest paid	(540)
Income taxes paid	(–)
Net cash flow from operating activities	22,600

Although you have used the indirect method, the figures for cash generated from operating activities and the net cash flow from operating activities are the same as those you calculated under the direct method.

6.7 FINALISING THE STATEMENT OF CASH FLOWS

We will now complete the final steps, which apply irrespective of which method you used to calculate the figures for the operating section of the statement of cash flows.

Step 5. Calculate the cash flow from investing activities. Start by identifying any changes in the company's holding of non-current assets, being careful to exclude any investments that are cash equivalents. Lily Soaps Ltd had no property, plant and equipment (PPE) on 1 January 2015, but at 31 December 2015 the carrying amount was £10,000. The annual charge for depreciation was £3,000 and this must be taken into account in order to calculate cash paid to acquire the assets. In this case, the result represents the net cash flows from investing activities (see Working 5).

Working 5	£
Closing carrying amount for PPE	10,000
Opening carrying amount for PPE	(–)
Depreciation for year	3,000
Carrying amount of PPE disposed during year	–
Cash flow from investing activities	13,000

Step 6. Calculate the cash flows from financing activities. This is straightforward because the opening share capital was the same as the closing share capital, but Lily Soaps Ltd obtained a £6,500 bank loan during the year. In this example, this figure represents the net cash flows from financing activities.

Step 7. Calculate the net increase or decrease in cash and cash equivalents by adding the results from steps 4, 5 and 6 (see Working 7).

Working 7	£
Net cash flow from operating activities	22,600
Net cash flow from investing activities	(13,000)
Net cash flows from financing activities	6,500
Increase in cash and cash equivalents	16,100

Step 8. Reconcile the net increase or decrease in cash and cash equivalents with the opening and closing figures in the statement of financial position. Lily Soaps Ltd had £10,000 in cash and cash equivalents on 1 January 2015 and increased it to £26,100 on 31 December 2015. The difference is £16,100 which balances with the calculations in Working 7.

We know from the statement of financial position that on 1 January 2015 Lily Soaps Ltd had cash and cash equivalents of £10,000 (the money Lily invested in the business), but at 31 December 2015 the cash and cash equivalents amounted to £26,100. Therefore, the business generated a net cash flow of £16,100 (£26,100 – £10,000) during the year. We now need to finalise the statement of cash flows to determine whether this increase in cash was the result of operating, investing or financing activities.

> **Activity**
> Prepare the statement of cash flows for Lily Soaps Ltd for the year ended 31 December 2015 using the indirect method, which is the one most widely used because it can be prepared from the statement of comprehensive income and the opening and closing statements of financial position.

Check your answer against the following statement of cash flows, which is based on the indirect method.

Lily Soaps Ltd Statement of cash flows for the year ended 31 December 2015	
	£
Cash flows from operating activities	
Profit before tax	29,900

(Continued)

Depreciation	3,000
Increase in inventory	(750)
Increase in trade receivables	(24,750)
Increase in prepaid expenses	(100)
Increase in trade payables	15,000
Increase in accrued expenses	300
Cash generated from operating activities	23,140
Interest paid	(540)
Income taxes paid	(–)
Net cash flow from operations	22,600
Cash flows from investing activities	
Acquisition of property, plant and equipment	(13,000)
Cash flows from financing activities	
Loan	6,500
Net increase in cash and cash equivalents	16,100
Cash and cash equivalents at 1 January 2015	10,000
Cash and cash equivalents at 31 December 2015	26,100

Now you have seen how to calculate the cash flows from investing and financing activities, you are ready to complete the statement of cash flows you started in section 6.5 using the direct method.

Activity
Prepare a complete statement of cash flows for Lily Soaps Ltd for the year ended 31 December 2015 using the direct method.

This should be easy as you calculated the cash flows from operating activities in section 6.5 and the cash flows from investing and financing activities are identical to those calculated in section 6.6. As you will see from the answer overleaf, the direct method is more informative than the indirect method and for this reason IAS 7 encourages reporting entities to use the direct method.

Lily Soaps Ltd	
Statement of cash flows for the year ended 31 December 2015	
	£
Cash flows from operating activities	
Cash receipts from customers	145,700
Cash paid to suppliers of goods and services	(108,060)
Cash paid to employees	(14,500)
Cash generated from operations	23,140
Interest paid	(540)
Income taxes paid	(–)
Net cash flow from operations	22,600
Cash flows from investing activities	
Acquisition of property, plant and equipment	(13,000)
Cash flows from financing activities	
Loan	6,500
Net increase in cash and cash equivalents	16,100
Cash and cash equivalents at 1 January 2015	10,000
Cash and cash equivalents at 31 December 2015	26,100

Irrespective of which method is used, the statement of cash flows shows that during the year Lily Soaps Ltd generated net cash inflows of £22,600 from its operating activities and £6,500 from its financing activities and this was more than sufficient to cover the net cash outflows of £13,000 from its investing activities. During the first year of trading, the company had generated a net increase in cash and cash equivalents of £16,100. Although there are cash and cash equivalents of £26,100 at the end of the period, Lily must remember that the company will need £8,970 of this to pay the current tax liability.

6.8   KEY POINTS

The statement of cash flows is the third of four financial statements that are prepared by reporting entities at the end of the accounting period. The purpose of the statement of cash flows is to provide historical information about changes in cash and cash equivalents resulting from the inflows and outflows of cash. Cash is essential to the survival of the business and this financial statement gives users important information about the entity's cash generating ability and its liquidity.

The preparation of this financial statement is guided by IAS 7, *Statement of Cash Flows* (IASB, 2012), which allows two methods for reporting the cash flows from operating activities: the direct method and the indirect method. Both methods result in the same figure for the net cash flows from operating activities. Although IAS 7 encourages the use of the direct method, because it supplies more relevant information and is more understandable to users, the indirect method is more commonly used. The presentation of the cash flows from investing and financing activities does not differ between the methods.

REVISION QUESTIONS

1. Explain the purpose of the statement of cash flows and differentiate between cash and cash equivalents.
2. Explain the difference between operating, investing and financing activities.
3. Compare and contrast the direct and indirect methods for presenting cash flows for operating activities.
4. The following financial statements relate to Beauty Plus Ltd.

Beauty Plus Ltd Statement of comprehensive income for the year ended 30 June 2016	
	£
Revenue	104,900
Cost of sales	(37,700)
Gross profit	67,200
interest received	100
Salaries	(30,000)
Rent and rates	(15,000)
Insurance	(3,000)
Lighting and heating	(1,500)
Telephone and internet	(2,000)
Advertising	(500)
Depreciation on equipment	(4,000)

(Continued)

Allowance for doubtful receivables	400
Operating profit	11,700
Income tax expense	(4,500)
Profit for the period	7,200

Beauty Plus Ltd				
Statements of financial position at 30 June				
		2016		2015
	£	£	£	£
ASSETS				
Non-current assets				
Property, plant and equipment		12,000		16,000
Current assets				
Inventory		12,000		10,000
Trade receivables	6,000		10,000	
Allowance for doubtful receivables	(600)		(1,000)	
Net trade receivables		5,400		9,000
Prepaid expenses		–		–
Cash and cash equivalents		15,300		8,000
		32,700		27,000
Total assets		44,700		43,000
EQUITY AND LIABILITIES				
Equity				
Share capital		(20,000)		(20,000)
Retained earnings		(12,200)		(5,000)
		(32,200)		(25,000)
Non-current liabilities				
Bank loan		–		(11,000)
Current liabilities				
Trade payables		(8,000)		(4,000)
Current tax liability		(4,500)		(3,000)
Total equity and liabilities		(44,700)		(43,000)

Additional information at 30 June 2016:

- There were no acquisitions or disposals of property, plant and equipment during the year and no accrued expenses.

Required
(a) Prepare a statement of cash flows for Beauty Plus Ltd for the year ended 30 June 2016 using the direct method.
(b) Prepare a statement of cash flows for Beauty Plus Ltd for the year ended 30 June 2016 using the indirect method.
(c) Comment on the net increase or decrease in cash and cash equivalents during the year and on whether it was the result of operating, investing or financing activities.

5. The following financial statements relate to Henley Ltd.

Henley Ltd Statement of comprehensive income for the year ended 31 December 2015	
	£
Revenue	120,000
Cost of sales	(60,000)
Gross profit	60,000
Employee salaries	(20,000)
Rent	(5,600)
Lighting and heating	(4,000)
Profit on disposal of property, plant and equipment	9,000
Depreciation on equipment	(8,000)
Allowance for doubtful receivables	(2,000)
Operating profit	29,400
Finance costs	(1,100)
Profit before tax	28,300
Income tax expense	(4,500)
Profit for the period	23,800

Henley Ltd
Statements of financial position at 31 December

	2015		2014	
	£	£	£	£
ASSETS				
Non-current assets				
Property, plant and equipment		20,000		16,000
Current assets				
Inventory		12,000		10,000
Trade receivables	30,000		10,000	
Allowance for doubtful receivables	(3,000)		(1,000)	
Net trade receivables		27,000		9,000
Prepaid expenses		–		–
Cash and cash equivalents		12,300		8,000
		51,300		27,000
Total assets		71,300		43,000
EQUITY AND LIABILITIES				
Equity				
Share capital		20,000		20,000
Retained earnings		22,800		5,000
		42,800		25,000
Non-current liabilities				
Bank loan		16,000		11,000
Current liabilities				
Trade payables		8,000		4,000
Accrued expenses		–		–
Current tax liability		4,500		3,000
Total equity and liabilities		71,300		43,000

The following information is also available at 31 December 2015:

- The company purchased £15,000 of property, plant and equipment during 2015.
- During 2015 equipment originally acquired for £5,000 was sold for £12,000. The accumulated depreciation on the equipment was £2,000 at the date of sale.
- Dividends of £6,000 were paid to shareholders on 1 July 2015.

Required

(a) Prepare a statement of cash flows for Henley Ltd for the year ended 31 December 2015 using the direct method.
(b) Prepare a statement of cash flows for Henley Ltd for the year ended 31 December 2015 using the indirect method.
(c) Review the cash flow position of Henley Ltd at 31 December 2015.

7

CONSOLIDATED FINANCIAL STATEMENTS

7.1 OBJECTIVES

This chapter focuses on the *consolidated financial statements* that are prepared for a group of companies following a business combination. After studying this chapter, you should be able to:

- Explain the purpose of consolidated financial statements.
- Describe the concept of control.
- Prepare a consolidated statement of financial position.
- Prepare a consolidated statement of comprehensive income.
- Prepare a consolidated statement of changes in equity.

7.2 PURPOSE OF CONSOLIDATED FINANCIAL STATEMENTS

Many large companies in the UK are the result of a *business combination*. A business combination is a transaction or other event in which an investor obtains control of one or more businesses (the investees). Mergers of equals are also business combinations. Examples of how a business combination can occur include transferring cash, incurring liabilities, issuing equity instruments or by contract alone. The business combination can be structured in various ways such as one entity becoming a subsidiary of another entity (the parent), the transfer of net assets from one entity to another entity or to a new entity. A subsidiary can be a company or an unincorporated entity.

The business combination must involve the acquisition of a business, which generally has three elements:

- Inputs – an economic resource that creates outputs when one or more processes are applied to it (eg non-current assets or intangible assets).

- Process – a system, standard, protocol, convention or rule that when applied to an input or inputs, creates outputs (for example strategic management or operational processes).
- Output – the result of inputs and processes applied to those inputs.

Definition

A business combination is a transaction or other event in which an acquirer obtains control of one or more businesses.

Source: IFRS 3, Appendix A (IASB, 2010b)

The purpose of consolidated financial statements is to present the assets, liabilities, equity, income, expenses and cash flows of the parent and its subsidiaries as if they were a single economic entity. IFRS 10, *Consolidated Financial Statements* (IASB, 2011b) requires a parent to prepare *consolidated financial statements* for the shareholders of the parent company, who will receive them in addition to the parent's financial statements. As the requirements of IAS 1, *Presentation of Financial Statements* (IASB 2011a) also apply, a complete set of consolidated financial statements includes:

- A consolidated statement of financial position.
- A consolidated statement of comprehensive income.
- A consolidated statement of changes in equity.
- A consolidated statement of cash flows.

A parent is not required to present consolidated financial statements if:

- It is a wholly-owned subsidiary or a partially-owned subsidiary of another entity and its other owners do not object to the parent not presenting consolidated financial statements.
- Its debt or equity instruments are not traded in a public market (in other words, it is not a listed company).
- It did not file, nor is it in the process of filing, its financial statements with a securities commission or other regulatory organisation for the purpose of issuing any class of instruments in a public market (in other words, it is not in the process of obtaining a listing).
- Its ultimate or any intermediate parent produces consolidated financial statements available for public use that comply with IFRSs.

7.3   CONTROL OF AN INVESTEE

Under IFRS 10, an investor determines whether it is a parent by assessing whether it controls one or more investees, and the investor must consider all the relevant facts and circumstances when making this assessment. An investor controls an investee when the investor possesses all the following elements of *control*:

- Power over the investee – The investor has existing rights that give it the ability to direct the relevant activities of the investee (the activities that significantly affect the investee's returns). Power arises from rights such as voting rights or rights resulting from contractual arrangements.
- Exposure to or rights to variable returns from its involvement with the investee – To exercise control over an investee, the investor must be exposed to or have rights to variable returns from its involvement with the investee. Variable returns are those that vary with the investee's performance. Therefore, they can be positive, negative, or both. Examples include changes in the value of the investor's investment, dividends and returns that are unavailable to other interest holders (such as cost savings or synergies obtained from interactions between the investor and investee).
- The ability to use its power over the investee to affect the amount of the investor's returns – A parent must also be able to use its power over the investee to influence its returns from its involvement with the investee.

Definitions

Control of an investee is achieved when the investor is exposed, or has rights, to variable returns from its involvement with the investee and has the ability to affect those returns through its power over the investee.

Power refers to existing rights [of the investor] that give the current ability to direct the relevant activities [of the investee].

Relevant activities are the activities of the investee that significantly affect the investee's returns.

Source: IFRS 10, Appendix A (IASB, 2011b)

When assessing whether an investor has *power* over an investee, the following sources of power must be considered:

- Voting rights.
- Potential voting rights that the holder could exercise (for example those obtained from a share option or convertible financial instrument).

- An investor's contractual and non-contractual rights (for example the ability to appoint an investee's key personnel or veto significant transactions).
- Special relationships between an investor and investee (for example the investee's operations may be dependent on the investor or its key personnel may also be employed by the investor).

Only substantive rights are capable of providing power. A right is substantive if it grants the holder the practical ability to exercise the right when decisions about the relevant activities of the investee need to be made. For example, the right of a lender to seize assets in the event of an investee defaulting on its debt is not substantive, as it does not give the lender power over the investee's relevant activities. In other cases, an investor might have power and secure *de facto* control over an investee due to:

- The size of its voting rights relative to the size and dispersion of other vote holders.
- Voting patterns and lack of attendance at the investee's previous shareholders' meetings.

Example
An investor must be able to influence returns through its power over the investee's decision making. This relationship between power and returns is an essential component of control under IFRS 10. In each of the following cases, the investor does *not* control the investee:

- Investor A has the power to direct the relevant activities of an investee, but has no right to a variable return from its involvement with the investee.
- Investor B receives a return from an investee but cannot use its power to direct the relevant activities of the investee.

Establishing an appropriate definition of control is more difficult than it first appears. For example, control can often be achieved without an investor possessing any direct legal ownership in the investee company. When an investor acquires an ownership interest in the ordinary share capital of another company it normally grants ownership over an equal proportion over the company's voting rights. Direct control is achieved if the investor acquires more than 50% of the investee's voting rights. A parent may exercise indirect control over a subsidiary through intermediate companies that are themselves controlled by the parent. Control does not always require possession of the majority of an investee's voting rights but depends on the size of the investor's voting rights relative to the size and dispersion of other vote holders. For example, an investor may hold 40% of the voting rights in an investee and the remaining voting rights are held by individual shareholders who have not participated in voting in the past. In this case, the 40% shareholder has *de facto* control.

Activity

Supermarket PLC acquires 48% of the voting rights of Grocer Ltd by purchasing 48% of Grocer's ordinary share capital. The remaining voting rights are held by 50,000 individual shareholders, none of whom hold more than 1% of the voting rights or make collective decisions. Indeed, none of them have voted at Grocer's previous shareholders' meetings.

Assess whether Supermarket PLC has control over Grocer Ltd, using the definition of control in IFRS 10 and the above information.

You need to remember that all three elements of control must be present:

- Although Supermarket does not control the majority of the voting rights in Grocer, it has power over Grocer's relevant activities. This power is obtained from the size of Supermarket's voting rights relative to the size and dispersion of the other vote holders. Supermarket's power is reinforced by the fact that the 50,000 other shareholders have never voted at a shareholders' meeting.
- Supermarket obtains variable returns from its investment, as its ownership of Grocer's ordinary shares provides dividends and a 48% share of any change in the value of Grocer.
- Supermarket has the power to influence its returns from Grocer by directing Grocer's relevant activities.

As all the elements of control exist, we can conclude that Supermarket PLC has control over Grocer Ltd, even though it has only 48% of Grocer's ordinary share capital. Note that the remaining 52% of Grocer's equity is referred to as the *non-controlling interest (NCI)*. Having control over Grocer means that Supermarket is the parent and must include this investee in the consolidated financial statements.

Definition

A non-controlling interest (NCI) is the equity in a subsidiary not attributable, directly or indirectly, to a parent.

Source: IFRS 3, Appendix A (IASB, 2010b)

7.4   CONSOLIDATED STATEMENT OF FINANCIAL POSITION AT ACQUISITION

Under IFRS 3, *Business Combinations* (IASB, 2010b), a business combination is accounted for at acquisition by preparing consolidated financial statements using the *acquisition method*:

- Identify the acquirer (the entity that obtains control of the acquiree).
- Determine the acquisition date (the date on which the acquirer obtains control of the acquiree).
- Recognise all identifiable assets acquired and liabilities assumed and measure them at acquisition-date fair value (there are exceptions for certain assets and liabilities). Measure any NCI at acquisition-date fair value or at the proportionate share of the acquiree's identifiable net assets (the difference between total assets and total liabilities).
- Recognise and measure goodwill or a gain from a bargain purchase. The consideration transferred consists of assets transferred, liabilities incurred, equity interests issued and contingent consideration. These are measured at acquisition-date fair value. Goodwill is calculated as follows:

$$\text{Goodwill} = \frac{\text{Consideration}}{\text{transferred}} + \frac{\text{Amount of}}{\text{NCI}} + \frac{\text{Fair value of previous}}{\text{equity interests}} - \frac{\text{Net assets}}{\text{recognised}}$$

If the difference is negative, the acquirer recognises a gain from a bargain purchase.

Definitions

Fair value is the price that would be received to sell an asset or paid to transfer a liability in an orderly transaction between market participants at the measurement date

Source: IFRS 13, Appendix A (IASB, 2011c)

Goodwill is an asset representing the future economic benefits arising from other assets acquired in a business combination that are not individually identified and separately recognised.

Source: IFRS 3, Appendix A (IASB, 2010b)

Example

On 31 January 2016 Forestry PLC paid £3.50 per share to acquire 100% of the £1 ordinary shares of Fencing Ltd. At this date all Fencing's assets and liabilities were valued at fair value. We will assume that the acquirer's share of the acquiree is the same as the percentage of ordinary shares acquired. The statements of financial position of the two companies at the date of acquisition were as follows.

Statements of financial position at 31 January 2016		
	Forestry PLC	Fencing Ltd
	£'000	£'000
ASSETS		
Non-current assets		
Property, plant and equipment	1,500	3,000
Investment in Fencing Ltd	3,500	–
	5,000	3,000
Current assets	1,000	1,000
Total assets	6,000	4,000
EQUITY AND LIABILITIES		
Equity		
Ordinary share capital	2,000	1,000
Retained earnings	2,000	2,000
	4,000	3,000
Current liabilities	2,000	1,000
Total equity and liabilities	6,000	4,000

There are five main stages in the consolidation process:

Step 1. Calculate whether control exists and establish the parent's proportional share of the subsidiary at the date of acquisition. Forestry PLC has taken control of Fencing by purchasing 100% of its ordinary share capital for £3.50 per share, so Fencing Ltd becomes a wholly-owned subsidiary of Forestry PLC.

Step 2. Calculate the fair value of the consideration transferred by the parent. An investor does not always use cash to invest in a subsidiary, so the consideration includes the fair value of any assets given, liabilities incurred or assumed, and the shares issued by the parent. The ordinary share capital of Fencing has a nominal value of £1 per share, so it has 1 million ordinary shares (£1m ordinary share capital ÷ £1 per share). At a purchase price of £3.50 per share, the fair value of the consideration transferred by Forestry PLC was £3.5m (1 million shares × £3.50 per share).

Step 3. Calculate the fair value of the subsidiary's assets and liabilities recognised at the date of acquisition. The assets and liabilities of Fencing were already valued at acquisition-date fair value. In exchange for the consideration transferred, Forestry obtains control over Fencing Ltd's identifiable net assets which had a fair value of £3m at the date of acquisition (£4m assets − £1m current liabilities).

Step 4. Calculate the NCI's proportionate share of the subsidiary's identifiable net assets at the date of acquisition. As Forestry PLC has acquired 100% of Fencing Ltd's ordinary share capital there is no NCI.

Step 5. Calculate the goodwill at the date of acquisition. The consideration transferred by Forestry was £0.5m more than the fair value of Fencing's identifiable net assets at the acquisition date (£3.5m consideration − £3m Fencing Ltd's net assets). As there is no NCI, this excess represents the goodwill:

	£'000
Fair value of the consideration transferred	3,500
Non-controlling interest at acquisition	−
Fair value of subsidiary's net assets at acquisition	(3,000)
Goodwill	500

Under the acquisition method, the subsidiary's assets, equity and liabilities are incorporated line by line into the consolidated statement of financial position through a process of elimination based on off-setting, leaving only the group's assets, equity and liabilities.

- The carrying amount of the parent's investment (the consideration transferred) is eliminated against the parent's share of the subsidiary's equity at the date of acquisition. Any excess is shown as goodwill. As a result, the investment in the subsidiary is replaced by the net assets that the parent has acquired.
- Any intra-group debts resulting from trading between entities in the group are eliminated by off-setting the amount payable by one entity against the amount receivable in the other. There are no intra-group items in this example.

Working 1 in the consolidated statement of financial position for Forestry PLC shows the elimination process. The £3.5m investment in Fencing Ltd is eliminated against Forestry's 100% share of Fencing's £3m equity at the acquisition date (£1m ordinary share capital + £2m retained earnings). After these amounts are eliminated, £0.5m of the investment remains. This is shown as goodwill under intangible non-current assets. The remaining assets and liabilities of Forestry PLC and Fencing Ltd (property, plant and equipment, current assets and current liabilities) are aggregated item by item to provide the figures for the consolidated statement of financial position.

You need to remember that we are using this layout to illustrate the consolidation process and the eliminations and workings are not published.

Forestry PLC Consolidated statement of financial position at 31 January 2016				
	Forestry PLC	Fencing Ltd	W1	Group
	£'000	£'000	£'000	£'000
ASSETS				
Non-current assets				
Property, plant and equipment	1,500	3,000	–	4,500
Investment in Fencing Ltd	3,500	–	(3,500)	
Intangible assets (goodwill)	–	–	500	500
	5,000	3,000	(3,000)	5,000
Current assets	1,000	1,000	–	2,000
Total assets	6,000	4,000	(3,000)	7,000
EQUITY AND LIABILITIES				
Equity				
Ordinary share capital	2,000	1,000	(1,000)	2,000
Retained earnings	2,000	2,000	(2,000)	2,000
	4,000	3,000	(3,000)	4,000
Current liabilities	2,000	1,000	–	3,000
Total equity and liabilities	6,000	4,000	(3,000)	7,000

In many business combinations, the parent acquires less than 100% of a subsidiary, as in the next example.

Example

On 30 April 2015, Maxi PLC paid £7.50 per share in order to acquire 90% of the 25p ordinary shares of Mini Ltd. The statements of financial position for each company at the date of acquisition are shown opposite.

Statements of financial position at 30 April 2015		
	Maxi PLC	Mini Ltd
	£'000	£'000
ASSETS		
Non-current assets		
Property, plant and equipment	2,600	3,000
Investment in Mini Ltd	5,400	–
	8,000	3,000
Current assets	1,500	1,200
Total assets	9,500	4,200
EQUITY AND LIABILITIES		
Ordinary share capital	2,500	200
Retained earnings	2,000	3,300
	4,500	3,500
Current liabilities	5,000	700
Total equity and liabilities	9,500	4,200

The following information about Mini Ltd's net assets is available at the date of acquisition:

- Freehold property with a carrying value of £1.8m had a market value of £2.9m.
- Current assets include £0.5m inventory with a net realisable value of only £250,000.

> **Activity**
> Work through the five steps and calculate the figures you need for the consolidated statement of financial position for Maxi PLC.

Check your answer against the following:

1. Maxi PLC acquired 90% of Mini Ltd. As Mini's £200,000 of ordinary share capital has a nominal value of 25p per share, the subsidiary has a total of 800,000 shares available for purchase. Maxi purchased 720,000 of these shares.
2. Maxi PLC purchased 90% of Mini Ltd's ordinary shares for £7.50 per share. The consideration transferred was £5.4m (720,000 shares × £7.50 per share).
3. Mini Ltd's identifiable net assets must be restated to their fair value at the date of acquisition. Before these adjustments, Mini's net assets had a carrying value

of £3.5m (total assets £4.2m – current liabilities £0.7m). At this date, Mini's net assets could also be measured using the £3.5m of total equity. The fair value adjustments to Mini's assets require the value of freehold property to be increased by £1m and a balancing revaluation reserve created in Mini's statement of financial position. In addition, current assets must be reduced by £250,000 to reflect the lower value of the inventory. This reduces Mini's retained earnings by £250,000. These fair value adjustments for Mini are shown below:

Mini's fair value adjustments	Original	Adjustment	Fair value
	£'000	£'000	£'000
ASSETS			
Non-current assets			
Property, plant and equipment	3,000	1,100	4,100
Current assets	1,200	(250)	950
Total assets	4,200	850	5,050
EQUITY AND LIABILITIES			
Equity			
Ordinary share capital	200	–	200
Retained earnings	3,300	(250)	3,050
Revaluation reserve	–	1,100	1,100
	3,500	850	4,350
Current liabilities	700	–	700
Total equity and liabilities	4,200	850	5,050

4. In this case there is a 10% NCI in Mini Ltd, which is measured as the proportionate share of the identifiable net assets (£4,350,000 × 10% = £435,000. This is included in the group statement of financial position under equity.
5. Goodwill on the acquisition of Mini Ltd is calculated as follows:

	£'000
Fair value of the consideration transferred	5,400
NCI at the acquisition date	435
Fair value of Mini's net assets at the acquisition date	(4,350)
Goodwill	1,485

> **Activity**
> Use your five workings to prepare a consolidated statement of financial position for Maxi PLC at 30 April 2015.

Remember to use the fair values you have calculated for Mini Ltd when preparing the consolidated statement of financial position. Start by eliminating Maxi PLC's investment of £5.4m against the 90% share (£3.915m) of the equity of Mini Ltd at the date of acquisition. The balancing figure (£1.485m) represents goodwill, which is recognised as an intangible non-current asset in the group accounts. The elimination process is shown overleaf in the column headed 'W1', where the total amount eliminated is £3.915m. The underlying calculations are as follows:

Maxi's share of Mini's equity at acquisition	£'000
Ordinary share capital (£200,000 × 90%)	180
Retained earnings (£3,050,000 × 90%)	2,745
Revaluation reserve (£1,100,000 × 90%)	990
Total equity (= Net assets acquired)	3,915

After the elimination process, the remaining 10% of Mini's equity and reserves represent the NCI in Mini. This is eliminated and shown in the group accounts as a NCI of £435,000. This adjustment is shown under column W2 of the solution. The underlying calculations are as follows:

10% NCI share of Mini's equity at acquisition	£'000
Ordinary share capital (£200,000 × 10%)	20
Retained earnings (£3,050,000 × 10%)	305
Revaluation reserve (£1,100,000 × 10%)	110
Total equity (= Net assets acquired)	435

The next step is to combine the individual figures for PPE, current assets and current liabilities for each entity. Remember that you should only include the equity of the parent and the NCI in the consolidated statement of financial position.

Now check your answer against the solution overleaf.

Maxi PLC
Consolidated statement of financial position at 30 April 2015

	Maxi PLC	Mini Ltd at fair value	W1	W2	Group
	£'000	£'000	£'000	£'000	£'000
ASSETS					
Non-current assets					
Property, plant and equipment	2,600	4,100	–	–	6,700
Investment in Mini Ltd	5,400	–	(5,400)	–	–
Intangible assets (goodwill)	–	–	1,485	–	1,485
	8,000	4,100	(3,915)	–	8,185
Current assets	1,500	950	–	–	2,450
	9,500	5,050	(3,915)	–	10,635
EQUITY AND LIABILITIES					
Equity					
Ordinary share capital	2,500	200	(180)	(20)	2,500
Retained earnings	2,000	3,050	(2,745)	(305)	2,000
Revaluation reserve	–	1,100	(990)	(110)	–
Non-controlling interest	–	–	–	435	435
	4,500	4,350	(3,915)	–	4,935
Current liabilities	5,000	700	–	–	5,700
Total equity and liabilities	9,500	5,050	(3,915)	–	10,635

7.5 CONSOLIDATED STATEMENT OF FINANCIAL POSITION AFTER ACQUISITION

We will now consider what happens after acquisition when the subsidiary continues to trade. The profit made by a subsidiary after acquisition represents the return on investment for the parent. Therefore, the parent's share of the post-acquisition profit is added to the group's retained earnings in the consolidated statement of financial position and the share of any NCI is added to the carrying amount of the NCI in the group accounts. If a subsidiary makes a post-acquisition loss, the same process applies in reverse. While a subsidiary's retained earnings are the most likely of its reserves to have changed since it was first acquired by its parent, it is possible that other reserves, such as the revaluation reserve, have changed. If so, these changes should be accounted for in the same way as movements in a subsidiary's post-acquisition retained earnings.

Another issue to consider is whether the goodwill recognised in the group accounts has suffered an impairment loss since the date of acquisition. Goodwill must be tested for any impairment loss at least annually. An impairment loss arises if the *recoverable amount* of the asset falls below its carrying amount. IFRS 36, *Impairment of Assets* (IASB, 2009a) defines the recoverable amount as the higher of its fair value less costs to sell, and its value in use. After acquisition, goodwill is shown in the group statement of financial position at cost less any accumulated impairment losses. Any impairment is recognised in the accounts and written off against the retained earnings of the group.

Example

One year has passed since Maxi PLC acquired 90% of Mini Ltd and the statements of financial position for the two companies are shown below. The statement of financial position for Mini Ltd at 30 April 2016 incorporates the fair value adjustments made on 30 April 2015.

Statements of financial position at 30 April 2016		
	Maxi PLC	Mini Ltd
	£'000	£'000
ASSETS		
Non-current assets		
Property, plant and equipment	2,900	4,400
Investment in Mini Ltd	5,400	–
	8,300	4,400
Current assets	1,500	1,050
Total assets	9,800	5,450
EQUITY AND LIABILITIES		
Equity		
Ordinary share capital	2,500	200
Retained earnings	2,500	3,550
Revaluation reserve	–	1,100
	5,000	4,850
Current liabilities	4,800	600
Total assets and liabilities	9,800	5,450

The following post-acquisition transactions and events took place during the year ending 30 April 2016:

- Maxi PLC and Mini Ltd each generated a profit of £500,000.
- Following an impairment review, it was found that the £1.485m goodwill arising on consolidation had suffered an impairment loss of 40% due to increased market competition.

Activity
Prepare a consolidated statement of financial position for Maxi PLC at 30 April 2016 that reflects the post-acquisition transactions and events.

Check your answer against the following solution, which shows the workings in columns W1–W4.

Maxi PLC Consolidated statement of financial position at 30 April 2016							
	Maxi PLC	Mini Ltd	W1	W2	W3	W4	Group
	£'000	£'000	£'000	£'000	£'000	£'000	£'000
ASSETS							
Non-current assets							
Property, plant and equipment	2,900	4,400	–	–	–	–	7,300
Investment in Mini Ltd	5,400	–	(5,400)	–	–	–	–
Intangible assets (goodwill)	–	–	1,485	–	–	(594)	891
	8,300	–	–	–	–	(594)	8,191
Current assets	1,500	1,050	–	–	–	–	2,550
Total assets	9,800	5,450	(3,915)	–	–	(594)	10,741
EQUITY AND LIABILITIES							
Equity							
Ordinary share capital	2,500	200	(180)	(20)	–	–	2,500
Retained earnings:							
Mini Ltd pre-acquisition	–	3,050	(2,745)	(305)	–	–	–

(Continued)

Maxi PLC's earnings and Mini Ltd's post-acquisition earnings	2,500	500	–	–	(50)	(594)	2,356
Revaluation reserve	–	1,100	(990)	(110)	–	–	–
Non-controlling interest	–	–	–	435		–	485
					50		
	5,000	4,850	(3,915)	–	–	(594)	5,341
Current liabilities	4,800	600	–	–	–	–	5,400
Total equity and liabilities	9,800	5,450	(3,915)	–	–	(594)	10,741

The group statement of financial position for Maxi PLC at 30 April 2016 reflects the impact of the combined business transactions for the post-acquisition period.

- Workings 1 and 2 are identical to the calculations for the consolidated statement of financial position at 30 April 2015. W1 shows the eliminations needed to recognise goodwill by eliminating Maxi's investment against its share of Mini's equity at the date of acquisition and W2 shows the adjustments needed to recognise the 10% NCI in Mini.
- W3 shows the adjustments needed to apportion Mini's post-acquisition profit (£500,000) between the group and the NCI. Mini's total equity has increased by £500,000 since being acquired by Maxi on 30 April 2015: 90% (£450,000) is allocated to the retained earnings of the group and 10% (£50,000) is added to the carrying value of the NCI. As a result, the carrying value of the NCI in the group increases to £485,000 (£435,000 at acquisition + £50,000 share of Mini's post-acquisition profit).
- W4 accounts for the 40% impairment of goodwill. The carrying value of goodwill is reduced by £594,000 (£1,485,000 x 40%). This amount is written off against the retained earnings of the group.

7.6 CONSOLIDATED STATEMENT OF COMPREHENSIVE INCOME

The *consolidated statement of comprehensive income* is usually provided instead of the parent's statement of comprehensive income. Under the *acquisition method,* all the subsidiary's revenue and expenses are incorporated line by line into the consolidated statement of comprehensive income. The main stages are:

Step 1. Eliminate intra-group sales by deducting from group revenue and deducting from group cost of sales. Deduct any unrealised profit on intra-group sales from closing inventory and add to group cost of sales.

Step 2. Cancel out other intra-group items, such as interest payable or management expenses

Step 3. Show any impairment loss on goodwill as an expense

Step 4. Deduct any profit after tax attributable to a NCI, leaving only the profit attributable to the group.

Step 5. Cancel out dividends paid by a subsidiary to its parent against dividends received by the parent. As you will see in the next section, the dividends paid to shareholders of the parent are shown in the *consolidated statement of changes in equity*.

Example

The statements of comprehensive income for Maxi PLC and Mini Ltd for the year ending 30 April 2016 are shown below.

Statements of comprehensive income for year ended 30 April 2016		
	Maxi PLC	*Mini Ltd*
	£'000	£'000
Revenue	2,200	2,000
Cost of sales	(700)	(800)
Gross profit	1,500	1,200
Administrative expenses	(400)	(300)
Distribution costs	(350)	(150)
Operating profit	750	750
Income tax expense	(250)	(250)
Profit for the period	500	500

The following transactions and events took place during the year ending 30 April 2016:

- Maxi sold Mini inventory at cost for £200,000 plus a mark-up of 50%. By the end of the year, this inventory had been sold by Mini.
- The group's goodwill of £1,485,000 suffered an impairment loss of 40%.

> **Activity**
> Prepare the consolidated statement of comprehensive income for the year end-ing 30 April 2016 for Maxi PLC.

Check your answer against the following solution.

Maxi PLC
Consolidated statement of comprehensive income for the year ending
30 April 2016

	Maxi PLC	Mini Ltd	W1	Group
	£'000	£'000	£'000	£'000
Revenue	2,200	2,000	(300)	3,900
Cost of sales	(700)	(800)	300	(1,200)
Gross profit	1,500	1,200	–	2,700
Administrative expenses	(400)	(300)	–	(700)
Distribution costs	(350)	(150)	–	(500)
Impairment of goodwill (W2)			–	(594)
Profit before tax	750	750	–	906
Income tax expense	(250)	(250)	–	(500)
Profit for the period	500	500	–	406
Profit attributable to:				
Non-controlling interest (W3)				50
Maxi PLC's shareholders (balancing figure)				356
Profit for the period				406

Many items in the individual statements of comprehensive income statement for the parent and subsidiary can be aggregated to provide the figures for the consoli-dated financial statement. However, you need to make three adjustments:

• W1 eliminates intra-group sales. The cost to Maxi of the inventory was £200,000 but Maxi added a 50% mark-up (£100,000) before selling it to Mini. Therefore, revenue is reduced by £300,000 (£200,000 + £100,000) to remove the intra-group revenue. An off-setting amount of £300,000 is deducted from group's cost of sales.

- W2 accounts for the 40% impairment to the £1,485,000 of goodwill on the acquisition of Mini Ltd. The impairment loss (£1,485,000 × 40% = £594,000) is included as an expense in the group statement of comprehensive income.
- W3 shows the division of the group's £406,000 profit for the period between the parent and the NCI. The shareholders owning the 10% NCI are entitled to 10% of Mini's profit (£500,000 × 10% = £50,000) and the balance of the group's profit is attributable to Maxi's shareholders (£406,000 − £50,000 = £356,000).

7.7   CONSOLIDATED STATEMENT OF CHANGES IN EQUITY

Although the parent, Maxi PLC, and the subsidiary, Mini Ltd, both achieved profits of £500,000 in the year after acquisition, the group profit was only £406,000 due to the impairment of goodwill. We can check whether the calculation of group profit is correct by preparing a *consolidated statement of changes in equity*. This shows the changes in equity and reserves during the period and provides a link between the consolidated statement of comprehensive income and the amount of equity shown in the consolidated statement of financial position.

In the following consolidated statement of changes in equity for the year ended 30 April 2016, the columns for share capital and retained earnings show the separate amounts attributable to shareholders of Maxi and the NCI. The balances at 30 April 2015 and 30 April 2016 are taken from the two consolidated statements of financial position you prepared in previous activities in this chapter. The figure of £406,000 for the consolidated comprehensive income for the year is correct because it matches the change in the group's total equity for the period (£5.341m at 30 April 2016 − £4.935m at 30 April 2015).

Maxi PLC					
Consolidated statement of changes in equity for the year ended 30 April 2016					
	Share capital	*Retained earnings*	*Total*	*NCI*	*Group*
	£'000	£'000	£'000	£'000	£'000
Balance at 30 April 2015	2,500	2,000	4,500	435	4,935
Comprehensive income for the period	–	356	356	50	406
Balance at 30 April 2016	2,500	2,356	4,856	485	5,341

7.8 KEY POINTS

A business combination is a transaction or other event in which an acquirer (the investor or parent) obtains control of one or more businesses (the investees or subsidiaries). Mergers of equals are also business combinations. Control of an investee is achieved when the investor is exposed to or has rights to variable returns from its involvement with the investee and has the ability to affect those returns through its power over the investee. A non-controlling interest (NCI) is the equity in a subsidiary not attributable, directly or indirectly, to a parent.

A parent is required to prepare *consolidated financial statements* for its shareholders. The purpose of consolidated financial statements is to present the assets, liabilities, equity, income, expenses and cash flows of the parent and its subsidiaries as if they were a single economic entity. At acquisition, the consolidated financial statements must be prepared using the acquisition method.

Consolidated financial statements reflect the economic substance of the group arrangement. The consolidated statement of comprehensive income is usually provided in the annual report and accounts instead of the parent's statement of comprehensive income. The consolidated statement of changes in equity shows the changes in equity and reserves during the period, thus providing a link between the consolidated statement of financial position and the consolidated statement of comprehensive income.

REVISION QUESTIONS

1. Explain how to determine whether a transaction is a business combination. In addition, describe the principle of control.
2. Explain the purpose of the consolidated financial statements and why goodwill is only shown in consolidated financial statements.
3. Explain why the net assets of a subsidiary should be adjusted to their fair value at the date of acquisition.
4. Polymatica PLC acquired 80% of Solutions Ltd for £500,000 on 1 July 2016. Solutions Ltd's net assets include property, plant and equipment, inventory and trade receivables with a total book value of £200,000 at the date of acquisition. Following independent appraisal of the PPE at the acquisition date, it was discovered that these assets had a fair value £100,000 greater than their book value.

Required

Calculate the following figures that will be shown in the consolidated statement of financial position for Polymatica PLC at the date of acquisition:

(a) the non-controlling interest
(b) goodwill

5. On 1 August 2015 Brewer Ltd paid £1.50 per share to acquire 40,000 of the £1 ordinary shares of Cooper Ltd. At this date, the share capital and reserves of Cooper Ltd were:

	£
£1 ordinary share capital	50,000
Retained earnings	16,250
Total	66,250

The statements of financial position for each company at 31 July 2016 were as follows:

	Brewer Ltd	Cooper Ltd
	£	£
ASSETS		
Non-current assets		
Property, plant and equipment	150,000	82,000
Investment in Cooper Ltd	60,000	
	210,000	
Current assets	195,000	92,250
Total assets	405,000	174,250
EQUITY AND LIABILITIES		
Equity		
Ordinary share capital	250,000	50,000
Retained earnings	32,000	36,250
Revaluation reserve		10,000
	282,000	96,250
Current liabilities	123,000	78,000
Total equity and liabilities	405,000	174,250

Following an impairment review on 31 July 2016, it was found that the goodwill arising on the business combination with Cooper Ltd had suffered an impairment loss of 50%.

Required

(a) Calculate the goodwill that will be paid by Brewer Ltd on the acquisition of Cooper Ltd.

(b) Prepare the consolidated statement of financial position for Brewer Ltd at 31 July 2016.

8

FINANCIAL STATEMENT ANALYSIS

8.1 OBJECTIVES

This chapter takes a user perspective and explains a technique for analyzing the main financial statements covered in this book. When you have studied this chapter, you should be able to:

- Explain the purpose of ratio analysis.
- Define and calculate the main investment and profitability ratios.
- Calculate the main liquidity, efficiency and gearing ratios.
- Interpret the meaning of these ratios.
- Discuss the limitations of ratio analysis.

8.2 PURPOSE OF RATIO ANALYSIS

The purpose of *ratio analysis* is to evaluate the financial performance and financial stability of a business using accounting ratios. The results of the analysis provide additional information that helps investors, lenders, creditors and other users of the financial statements make their different economic decisions. A ratio describes a quantitative relationship between two data items and is usually presented as $x\%$ or $x{:}1$. In some cases it is presented in monetary terms, such as x pence per share.

A ratio is a useful measure because it can be compared with:

- Budgets and plans for the period (internal users only).
- Previous periods for the same business.
- Other businesses in the same sector (inter-firm comparison).
- Industry benchmarks (published averages for the sector).

> **Definition**
> Ratio analysis is the use of accounting ratios to evaluate a company's operating performance and financial stability… In conducting an analysis comparisons will be made with other companies and with industry averages over a period of time. The analysis of ratios can indicate how well a company is run, the risks of financial insolvency, and the financial returns provided.
>
> Source: Law, 2010, p. 345

There are four main types of ratio and each has a specific purpose:

- *Investment ratios* are used for evaluating shareholders' return.
- *Profitability ratios* are used for assessing the operating performance of the business.
- *Liquidity and efficiency ratios* are used for evaluating the solvency, financial stability and management of working capital of the business.
- *Gearing ratios* are used for examining the financial structure of the business and assessing financial risk.

Any number of ratios can be calculated and the choice depends on the needs of the user and the availability of relevant data. This chapter illustrates some of the most widely used ratios (see Figure 8.1). As there are no standard definitions of the terms used in the formulae, care must be taken when comparing the ratios you have calculated with ratios from other sources, which may have been calculated on a different basis.

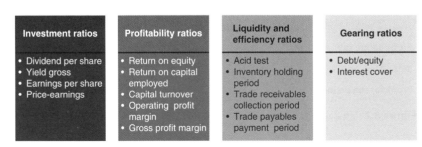

Figure 8.1 Main types of ratio

Ratios can be applied to the financial statements of any size and type of business. We are going to apply them to the consolidated financial statements of Ted Baker PLC, a group company that is listed on the London Stock Exchange. Extracts from the group financial statements are reproduced in Figure 8.2. You will see that Ted Baker has published a separate statement of income and statement of comprehensive income, and refers to the statement of financial position as the balance sheet, which reflects the traditional UK terminology.

Group Income Statement

For the 52 weeks ended 25 January 2014	Note	2014	2013
		£'000	£'000
Revenue	2	321,921	254,466
Cost of sales		(123,451)	(95,740)
Gross profit		**198,470**	**158,726**
Distribution costs		(123,211)	(101,357)
Administrative expenses		(43,381)	(32,984)
Exceptional costs		(1,046)	(2,614)
Licence income		8,888	7,509
Other operating income		(132)	234
Operating profit		**39,588**	**29,514**
Finance income	4	316	34
Finance expenses	4	(1,312)	(824)
Share of profit of jointly controlled entity, net of tax	12	331	198
Profit before tax	3,6	**38,923**	**28,922**
Income tax expense	6	(10,071)	(7,325)
Profit for the period		**28,852**	**21,597**

Figure 8.2 Ted Baker PLC Report and Accounts 2014 (extract)

(Continued)

Group Statement of Comprehensive Income

For the 52 weeks ended 25 January 2014	Note	2014	2013
		£'000	£'000
Profit for the period		**28,852**	**21,597**
Other comprehensive income			
Net effective portion of changes in fair value of cash flow hedges		(2,486)	(320)
Net change in fair value of cash flow hedges transferred to profit or loss		545	723
Exchange differences on translation of foreign operations net of tax		(3,276)	152
Other comprehensive income for the period		**(5,217)**	**555**
Total comprehensive income for the period		**23,635**	**22,152**

Group Balance Sheet

At 25 January 2014	Note	2014	2013
		£'000	£'000
Non-current assets			
Intangible assets	10	6,080	983
Property, plant and equipment	11	45,083	45,412
Investment in equity accounted investee	12	1,024	693
Deferred tax assets	13	4,450	4,523
Prepayments		564	674
		57,201	**52,285**

(Continued)

Figure 8.2 (Continued)

Current assets			
Inventories	14	80,432	67,673
Trade and other receivables	15	34,793	34,124
Amount due from equity accounted investee	12	164	225
Derivative financial assets	16	499	544
Cash and cash equivalents	17	28,521	9,823
		144,409	**112,389**
Current liabilities			
Trade and other payables	18	(45,289)	(40,793)
Bank overdraft	17	(37,282)	(19,862)
Income tax payable		(3,857)	(4,360)
Derivative financial liabilities	16	(3,118)	(269)
		(89,546)	**(65,284)**
Non-current liabilities			
Deferred tax liabilities	13	–	(497)
		–	**(497)**
Net assets		**112,064**	**98,893**
Equity			
Share capital	19	2,194	2,160
Share premium account	19	9,139	9,137
Other reserves	19	(1,850)	91
Translation reserve	19	(2,980)	296
Retained earnings	19	105,561	87,209
Total equity attributable to equity shareholders of the parent company		**112,064**	**98,893**
Total equity		**112,064**	**98,893**

(Continued)

Selected notes (extracts)	2014	2013
4 Of which, interest payable (£'000)	(1,279)	(646)
8 Total dividends for the period (£'000)	14,708	11,329
9 Weighted number of ordinary shares ('000)	43,497	43,282
15 Of which, trade receivables (£'000)	23,105	19,529
18 Of which, trade payables (£'000)	(22,049)	(22,097)
20 Weighted average share price (pence)*	1,090.7	688.4
20 Maximum risk free interest rate (%)*	2.77	4.60

*Note to readers: These notes are taken from different pages of the accounts. In the following discussion, the relevant note will be clear from the context.

Figure 8.2 Ted Baker PLC Report and Accounts 2014 (extract)

8.3 INVESTMENT RATIOS

We start the analysis from an investor perspective, since existing and potential investors are the first of the primary user groups (IASB, 2010a). We will examine four *investment ratios* that are widely used to evaluate shareholders' return and aid investment decisions.

Dividend per share

The *dividend per share* measures the amount of dividend paid on one ordinary share during the year. You will remember that dividends are a distribution of part of the earnings of the entity to its ordinary shareholders. Therefore, dividends represent a portion of the return to shareholders on their investment that is paid in cash. At the end of the year, the directors make a decision about how much of the current year's earnings will be kept in the business to help it grow and how much will be distributed as dividends. The directors will want to increase the dividend or at least keep it stable in order to satisfy existing shareholders and attract new investors. Therefore, during times of economic recession when profits may be relatively low, the directors may decide to use some of the retained profits to maintain dividend levels. Dividend per share is expressed in pence and is calculated using the formula:

$$\text{Dividend per share} = \frac{\text{Dividends}}{\text{Number of ordinary shares}} \quad [\times 100 \text{ for pence}]$$

The data you need for this ratio are given in Notes 8 and 9 below the financial statements in Figure 8.2. Using that information, we calculated the total dividends for the period as follows:

	2014	2013
	£'000	£'000
Interim dividend	4,145	7,965
Final dividend	10,563	3,364
Total dividends	14,708	11,329

	2014	2013
Dividend per share =	$\dfrac{£14,708k}{43,497k} \times 100 = 33.81p$	$\dfrac{£11,329k}{43,282k} \times 100 = 26.17p$

The dividend per share increased by just over 7p in 2014 compared to 2013. This reflects the increased proportion of total dividends to the number of ordinary shares. This is good news for existing investors and will help attract new investors.

Dividend yield

Dividend yield builds on the dividend per share and measures the dividend yielded on one ordinary share in relation to the average share price over the year. The ratio is shown as a percentage and is calculated using the formula:

$$\text{Dividend yield} = \frac{\text{Dividend per share}}{\text{Average share price}} \quad [\times 100 \text{ for \%}]$$

You have just calculated the dividend per share and you can obtain the average share price from Note 20 in Figure 8.2. The workings are as follows:

$$\text{Dividend yield} = \begin{array}{c} 2014 \\ \dfrac{33.81\text{p}}{1,090.7\text{p}} \times 100 = 3.1\% \end{array} \qquad \begin{array}{c} 2013 \\ \dfrac{26.17\text{p}}{688.4\text{p}} \times 100 = 3.8\% \end{array}$$

These results show a slight decrease in dividend yield in 2014 compared with 2013, but it is due to the large increase in the average share price, which reflected rising optimism in the stock market as the economic recession began to recede. Although the dividend per share had increased over the period, it was proportionately smaller because it would take some time for the improving economy to be reflected in higher profits.

Earnings per share

So far we have only looked at ratios that reflect that part of profit distributed to shareholders as dividends. However, the directors retain some of the profit earned during the year to invest in new assets to help the business earn more profits in the future. This retained profit also belongs to the shareholders, so total profit comprises dividends plus retained earnings. By focusing on total profit, *earnings per share (EPS)* measures the shareholders' total return earned by one ordinary share. It is shown in pence and is calculated using the formula:

$$\text{Earnings per share} = \frac{\text{Profit for ordinary shareholder}}{\text{Number of ordinary shares}} \ [\times 100 \text{ for pence}]$$

> **Activity**
> Calculate Ted Baker's earnings per share for ordinary shareholders for 2014 and compare it with 2013.

The figures you need are the profit for the period, which is the profit after interest and tax, and the average number of ordinary shares, which you used in one of the ratios you calculated earlier. The workings are as follows:

$$\text{Earnings per share} = \begin{array}{c} 2014 \\ \dfrac{£28,852\text{k}}{43,497\text{k}} \times 100 = 66.33\text{p} \end{array} \qquad \begin{array}{c} 2013 \\ \dfrac{£21,597\text{k}}{43,282\text{k}} \times 100 = 49.9\text{p} \end{array}$$

EPS is a measure on which many shareholders place considerable weight. In the case of Ted Baker's, the results show an increase of just over 16p in 2014 compared with 2013, which reflected the increased profitability. It is important to remember that EPS is a measure of the entity's performance and it is not an amount of money distributed to shareholders. The ratio that shows the amount of money paid on one share is the dividend per share. EPS is always higher than the dividend per share because EPS is based on the total profit for the year: dividends plus retained earnings.

In order to aid comparison of performance, IAS 33, *Earnings per share* (IASB, 2003b) sets out the principles for determining and presenting EPS. The standard requires the basic and diluted EPS to be shown in the statement of comprehensive income, giving equal prominence for all periods presented. This information was deliberately excluded from Figure 8.2 so that you could learn how to calculate this important ratio. We have calculated the diluted EPS, which takes account of dilutive options and events after the balance sheet date that may affect the EPS.

Price-earnings ratio

The *price-earnings (P/E)* ratio compares the amount invested in one share with the EPS and reflects the stock market's view on how long the current level of EPS will be sustained. It is measured in years and is calculated using the formula:

$$P/E = \frac{\text{Share price}}{\text{Earnings per share}}$$

> **Activity**
> Calculate Ted Baker's P/E ratio for 2014 and compare with 2013.

Check your answer against the following solution:

2014	2013

$$P/E = \frac{1{,}090.7p}{66.33p} = 16.44 \text{ years} \qquad \frac{688.4p}{49.9p} = 13.80 \text{ years}$$

The higher P/E ratio in 2014 indicates that the stock market was more confident about how long the current level of EPS would be sustained than it was in 2013, and reflects the general optimism in the stock market as many economies moved out of the economic recession. As you can see, the length of time increased by nearly 3 years. This suggests that shareholders were optimistic about the future and therefore they might be willing to pay more for the Group's shares than was justified by the current level of earnings.

8.4 PROFITABILITY RATIOS

Profitability ratios are used by internal and external users to assess how effective the directors have been in managing the business in terms of generating income and controlling costs. Not only are investors, lenders and creditors interested in the profitability of the business, but also employees, major suppliers and customers.

Return on equity

The *return on equity (ROE)* is of particular interest to investors because it focuses on the profit generated on the investment of shareholders' funds. This helps them assess the stewardship of management. The ratio focuses solely on shareholders' equity and ignores any long-term finance shown under non-current liabilities. For this ratio we will define 'return' as the profit for ordinary shareholders. It is calculated using the formula:

$$\text{ROE} = \frac{\text{Profit for ordinary shareholders}}{\text{Equity}} \; [\times 100 \text{ for } \%]$$

> **Activity**
> Calculate Ted Baker's ROE for 2014 and compare with 2013.

The two figures you need are the profit for the period, which represents the profit after interest and tax, and the total equity. Check your results against the following solution:

2014	2013

$$\text{ROE} = \frac{£28,852\text{k}}{£112,064\text{k}} \times 100 = 25.75\% \quad \frac{£21,597\text{k}}{£98,893\text{k}} \times 100 = 21.84\%$$

The results provide good news for investors as the ROE improved in 2014 when it represented £25.75 for every £100 of equity, compared to £21.84 the previous year. The return in 2014 was considerably higher than the maximum risk free interest rate of 2.77% shown in Note 20.

Return on capital employed

The *return on capital employed (ROCE)* measures the percentage return on the total funds used to finance the business. This provides useful information about management's effectiveness in generating income from all the resources and controlling costs. For this ratio we will define 'return' as the operating profit, which is the profit before interest and tax, and 'capital employed' as equity plus non-current liabilities. This means we will include the shareholders' funds and all long-term debts which represent additional sources of finance to the business since cash is not needed to pay them immediately. The ratio is calculated using the formula:

$$\text{ROCE} = \frac{\text{Operating profit}}{\text{Equity} + \text{Non-current liabilities}} \, [\times \, 100 \text{ for } \%]$$

> **Activity**
> Calculate Ted Baker's ROCE for 2014 and compare with 2013.

Finding the operating profit should be straightforward, but you need to calculate the capital employed by adding total equity to the total for non-current liabilities, ignoring the negative sign on the total non-current liabilities. Check your answer against the following workings.

	2014	2013
	£'000	£'000
Equity	112,064	98,893
Non-current liabilities	–	497
Capital employed	112,064	99,390

2014	2013
$\text{ROCE} = \dfrac{£39,588k}{£112,064k} \times 100 = 35.33\%$	$\dfrac{£29,514k}{£99,390k} \times 100 = 29.70\%$

The increased capital in 2014 gave proportionately higher profits and the results show an improvement in the ROCE of just over 5% compared with 2013. This suggests the directors have been using the entity's resources effectively to generate income and they have also been able to control costs. ROCE should reflect the element of risk in the investment and can be compared with interest rates for other investments where there is barely any risk, such as bank deposit rates. In this case, the return in 2014 is well above the maximum risk free interest rate of 2.77% shown in Note 20.

If you compare the values you calculated for ROCE with those you calculated for ROE, you will see that the ROE shows a more modest return. This is because ROCE does not take account of the obligation the business has to service and repay long-term debt. The definition of 'capital employed' we used for the ROCE was equity plus non-current assets, which is the same as total assets minus current liabilities. Comparing the two ratios:

$$\text{ROCE} = \frac{\text{Operating profit}}{\text{Equity} + \text{Non-current liabilities}} \quad \begin{array}{l}\text{(Profit before finance expenses)} \\ \text{(Total assets minus current liabilities)}\end{array}$$

$$\text{ROE} = \frac{\text{Profit for ordinary shareholders}}{\text{Equity}} \quad \begin{array}{l}\text{(Profit after finance expenses)} \\ \text{(Total assets minus total liabilities)}\end{array}$$

ROCE is referred to as the prime ratio because it is related to two subsidiary ratios: capital turnover and operating profit margin. These two ratios show how this profitability has been achieved and how it can be improved. We will look at capital turnover next.

Capital turnover

Capital turnover measures the number of times capital employed was used during the year to achieve the revenue. The formula is:

$$\text{Capital turnover} = \frac{\text{Revenue}}{\text{Equity} + \text{Non-current liabilities}}$$

> **Activity**
> Calculate Ted Baker's capital turnover for 2014 and compare with 2013.

Finding the figure for revenue should be straightforward and you have already calculated the figure for capital employed, so all you need to do is insert them in the formula as follows:

2014	2013
$\text{Capital turnover} = \dfrac{£321,921k}{£112,064k} = 2.87 \text{ times}$	$\dfrac{£254,466k}{£99,390k} = 2.56 \text{ times}$

The level of activity should be as high as possible for the lowest level of investment. In this case, the capital employed in the business was turned over more than 2½ times in both years to achieve the revenue. The higher ratio for 2014 suggests more efficient use of capital employed, resulting in increased sales volume. In addition, it is worth noting that although total equity has increased (mainly due to the previous year's retained earnings), there were no non-current liabilities in 2014.

Operating profit margin

The *operating profit margin* measures the percentage return on revenue based on the operating profit. The ratio is calculated using the formula:

$$\text{Operating profit margin} = \frac{\text{Operating profit}}{\text{Revenue}} \; [\times 100 \text{ for } \%]$$

Activity
Calculate Ted Baker's operating profit margin for 2014 and compare with 2013.

All you need to do is identify the figures in the income statement. Check your calculations against the following workings:

	2014	2013

$$\text{Operating profit margin} = \frac{£39,588k}{£321,921k} \times 100 = 12.3\% \qquad \frac{£29,514k}{£254,466k} \times 100 = 11.6\%$$

The results show a slight improvement in operating profit margin in 2014 when it represented an operating profit of £12.30 on every £100 of revenue. The improvement in 2014 suggests higher selling prices and/or better control of operating costs.

The last three ratios we have looked at are interrelated:

$$\text{Capital turnover} \times \text{Operating profit margin} = \text{ROCE}$$

We can test this by inserting the ratios we have calculated for Ted Baker (minor differences are due to rounding):

2014	2013
$2.87\% \times 12.3\% = 35.3\%$	$2.56\% \times 11.6\% \times = 29.7\%$

A business can improve ROCE (the prime ratio) by reducing costs and/or raising selling prices if that is feasible, and this will improve its operating profit margin. Alternatively, it can increase its sales volume and/or reduce its capital employed, which will improve its capital turnover.

Gross profit margin

For businesses in the retail sector in particular, the gross profit is considered to be an essential feature of management control and a guide to pricing and purchasing policies. The *gross profit margin* measures the percentage on revenue based on the operating profit. The ratio is calculated using the formula:

$$\text{Gross profit margin} = \frac{\text{Gross profit}}{\text{Revenue}} \; [\times 100 \text{ for } \%]$$

> **Activity**
> Calculate Ted Baker's gross profit margin for 2014 and compare it with 2013.

The figures you need are given in the income statement, so all you need to do is insert them into the formula as follows:

	2014	2013

$$\text{Gross profit margin} = \frac{£198,470k}{£321,921k} \times 100 = 61.65\% \qquad \frac{£158,726k}{£254,466k} \times 100 = 62.38\%$$

As you can see, the gross profit margin was similar in both years, with the business making a slightly smaller gross profit of £61.65 on every £100 of revenue in 2014. This suggests lower selling prices and/or weaker control over the cost of sales. The gross profit margin is much higher than the operating profit margin because the gross profit only takes account of revenue and the cost of sales. On the other hand, the operating profit takes account of revenue, licence income and other operating income, and all the operating costs (cost of sales, the distribution costs, administrative expenses and exceptional costs).

8.5   LIQUIDITY AND EFFICIENCY RATIOS

Liquidity ratios are used to evaluate the solvency and financial stability of a business and are therefore relevant to all users who have an interest in whether the business is a going concern. The liquidity of the business is of particular importance to lenders and creditors who need to assess whether the business is able to service loans and pay for goods and services bought on credit. *Efficiency ratios* (also known as *funds management ratios*) are used to assess how effectively the directors have managed the *working capital* (the current assets and current liabilities) of the business.

Current ratio and the acid test

The *current ratio* is a liquidity ratio that measures the relationship between current assets and short-term liabilities and is expressed as *x*:1. The formula is:

$$\text{Current ratio} = \frac{\text{Current assets}}{\text{Current liabilities}}$$

The *acid test* is more stringent and measures the relationship between the liquid assets and short-term liabilities. We will define 'liquid assets' as current assets minus inventories, as inventory cannot be converted into cash at short notice. The formula is:

$$\text{Acid test} = \frac{\text{Current assets} - \text{Inventories}}{\text{Current liabilities}}$$

Activity

Calculate Ted Baker's current ratio and acid test for 2014 and compare with 2013.

The figures you need are disclosed in Ted Baker's balance sheet, so all you need to do is insert them into each formula as follows:

2014   2013

$$\text{Current ratio} = \frac{£144,409\text{k}}{£89,546\text{k}} = 1.61:1 \qquad \frac{£112,389\text{k}}{£65,284\text{k}} = 1.72:1$$

2014   2013

$$\text{Acid test} = \frac{£144,409\text{k} - £80,432\text{k}}{£89,546\text{k}} = 0.71:1 \qquad \frac{£112,389\text{k} - £67,673\text{k}}{£65,284\text{k}} = 0.68:1$$

The results demonstrate that the ratios are stable. In 2014 Ted Baker had £1.61 of current assets and £0.71 of liquid assets for every £1 of current liabilities. Although both ratios are slightly lower than in the previous year, the Group would have no difficulty in paying all current creditors in the unlikely event that they all demanded immediate payment. These results assure users that the business is a going concern.

A ratio of less than 1:1 is not necessarily a cause for concern. You need to remember that the accounts are prepared on a prudent basis, which means that all possible costs and losses are accrued even if the amounts are based on estimates. In addition, different items of trade payables shown in Ted Baker's balance sheet will be due for payment at different times during the next financial year. It is also good funds management for a business to give a shorter credit period to customers than the period agreed with suppliers. For example, some businesses offer their customers 30 days to pay, but negotiate 90 days' credit from their suppliers. Such a trading policy would result in lower trade receivables (which are part of current assets) than trade payables (which are part of current liabilities) at the end of the year. It is difficult to generalise about ideal levels of liquidity, but in many industries there are benchmarks of what is considered to be a good acid test ratio.

Inventory holding period

The *inventory holding period* is an efficiency ratio that measures the average period between purchase and sale (or use) of inventory over the year. We will use a formula that calculates the ratio in months:

$$\text{Inventory holding period} = \frac{\text{Inventory}}{\text{Cost of sales}} \ [\times\ 12 \text{ for months}]$$

Ideally we should use the average inventory:

$$\frac{\text{Opening inventory} + \text{Closing inventory}}{2}$$

Since closing inventory for one year is opening inventory for the next, we would be able to calculate the average inventory for 2014. However, we do not have the opening inventory for the previous year, so we will define inventory as 'closing inventory' to allow us to compare the ratios for the two years.

Activity
Calculate Ted Baker's inventory holding period for 2014 and compare it with 2013.

You need to identify the figures for inventories in the Group's balance sheet (statement of financial position) and the cost of sales figures from the income statement. Check your results against the following workings.

	2014	2013
Inventory holding period $=$	$\dfrac{£80,432k}{£123,451k} \times 12 = 7.82$ months	$\dfrac{£67,673k}{£95,740k} \times 12 = 8.48$ months

In general, the shorter the period of time that inventories are held the better to keep storage costs to the minimum and to reduce the risk of damage, wastage and obsolescence. The results show a slight improvement in 2014 because management moved inventory faster than in 2013. In both years, you can see that on average it took more than 6 months (one fashion season) to sell (or use) the inventories. However, this is not a major cause for concern as sales of some products may straddle the seasons.

Trade receivables collection period

The *trade receivables collection period* is an efficiency ratio that measures the average time customers took to pay for goods and services bought on credit over the year. We will use a formula that calculates the ratio in months:

$$\text{Trade receivables collection period} = \frac{\text{Trade receivables}}{\text{Revenue}} \times 12$$

> **Activity**
> Calculate Ted Baker's trade receivables collection period for 2014 and compare it with 2013.

You will find the data you need for trade receivables in the extract from Note 15 below the financial statements in Figure 8.2. You identified the figure for revenue in an earlier activity. Check your answer against the following workings:

	2014	2013

$$\text{Trade receivables collection period} = \frac{£23,105k}{£321,921k} \times 12 = 0.86 \text{ months} \qquad \frac{£19,529k}{£254,466k} \times 12 = 0.92 \text{ months}$$

The results demonstrate the ratios are stable and the average period customers took to settle their debts was just under 1 month. If the Group's policy is to give customers 1 month's credit, then this suggests management has an efficient system of credit control. However, we would need to confirm this assumption before drawing firm conclusions.

Trade payables payment period

The *trade payables payment period* is an efficiency ratio that measures the average time the business took to pay for goods and services purchased on credit from trade suppliers over the year. We use a formula that calculates the ratio in months:

$$\text{Trade payables payment period} = \frac{\text{Trade payables}}{\text{Cost of sales}} \times 12$$

Ideally we should use purchases, but as this is not disclosed we will use cost of sales. This is an inferior proxy because it is affected by fluctuations in inventory levels, but as long as we are consistent, it is possible to draw conclusions from it.

> **Activity**
> Calculate Ted Baker's trade payables payment period for 2014 and compare it with 2013.

You will find the data you need for trade payables in Note 18 below the financial statements in Figure 8.2. You identified the figure for cost of sales in an earlier activity. Check your results against the following workings.

2014	2013

$$\text{Trade payables payment period} = \frac{£22,049k}{£123,451k} \times 12 = 2.14 \text{ months} \qquad \frac{£22,097k}{£95,740k} \times 12 = 2.77 \text{ months}$$

The interpretation of the results depends on the length of credit period agreed with trade suppliers. If the Group had an average credit period of 3 months, then the results demonstrate good funds management because the Group is making use of the time allowed to pay and there is no risk of having to pay interest on late payments or jeopardising relationships with suppliers. However, it is difficult to draw firm conclusions without details of the average length of time agreed with suppliers.

Some people do not like getting into debt and prefer to pay invoices straight away, rather than wait until they are due. However, this is not a good way of managing cash in a business because receiving goods and services on credit is equivalent to being given an interest-free loan. In a business context, if suppliers do not give credit, the business may have to go into overdraft to pay cash for the goods and services. This does not mean that a business should wait until it receives a solicitor's letter or risk supplies being cut off, but the credit controller should take the maximum time allowed to pay suppliers whilst collecting money from customers as quickly as possible. This is what Ted Baker appears to be doing and suggests efficient financial management.

8.6   GEARING RATIOS

Gearing (or *leverage*) refers to the relationship between equity and long-term debt finance in the business. The financial structure of a business can have an impact on its financial performance and gearing ratios are used by investors and lenders to assess financial risk when a business has an obligation to service and repay long-term debt(s).

Debt/equity ratio

The *debt/equity ratio* focuses on the statement of financial position and describes the financial structure of the business in terms of the proportion of long-term debt to shareholders' funds. There are a number of ways in which *debt* can be defined, but we will define it as non-current liabilities. The ratio is shown as a percentage and can be calculated using the formula:

$$\text{Debt/equity ratio} = \frac{\text{Non-current liabilities}}{\text{Equity}} \; [\times 100 \text{ for \%}]$$

Activity
Calculate Ted Baker's debt/equity ratio for 2014 and compare it with 2013.

You should have had little difficulty with this because both figures are shown in the Group's balance sheet. Check your answer against the following solution.

	2014	2013

$$\text{Debt/equity ratio} = \frac{£0k}{£112,064k} \times 100 = 0\% \qquad \frac{£497k}{£98,893k} \times 100 = 0.5\%$$

The general interpretation is that the higher the gearing, the higher the risk that the business will be unable to pay the interest on its loans or make repayments when profits are low. On the other hand, the higher the gearing, the higher the returns will be to shareholders in strong economic conditions. You may be surprised by the 0% gearing in 2014 and the very low gearing in 2013 (£0.50 of long-term debt for every £100 of equity). However, this is a very good sign because it means that the financial structure does not increase the risk to lenders or investors.

Interest cover

Interest cover is a gearing ratio that focuses on the income statement (or statement of comprehensive income if the entity adopts a single statement approach). It assesses the relative safety of interest payments by measuring the number of times interest payable on long-term debt is covered by the available profits. This avoids problems relating to the different ways in which debt can be defined. The ratio can be calculated using the formula:

$$\text{Interest cover} = \frac{\text{Operating profit}}{\text{Interest payable}}$$

Interest payable is one of the finance expenses and you will find the data you need in the extract from Note 4 below the financial statements in Figure 8.2.

$$\text{Interest cover} = \frac{\text{£39,588k}}{\text{£1,279k}} = 30.95 \text{ times} \qquad \frac{\text{£29,514k}}{\text{£646k}} = 45.69 \text{ times}$$

2014 | 2013

Interest cover was lower in 2014 than in 2013 because interest payable was proportionately higher than profit before interest and tax. However, interest payable in 2014 was covered by operating profit more than 30 times, which seems very safe. This means there is low risk to lenders and/or long-term creditors that the Group would be unable to service its long-term debts.

If we had the data, it would be useful to analyse all the gearing ratios over a longer period of time to identify the trend. We could also compare them with Ted Baker's competitors and with industry benchmarks.

8.7   TREND ANALYSIS

If we had the data for previous years, it would be useful to calculate all the ratios that we have examined for Ted Baker over an extended period. This is known as trend analysis. Table 8.1 shows Ted Baker's operating profit margin over the ten years that span the period before the downturn in the global economy in 2007 and the years of the recession (late 2007 to 2013). You can see that the trend was stable until 2009, when the economic recession began to hit Ted Baker's profit margin, and by the start of 2014 it had still not returned to the pre-recession level. The ratios for the last few years suggest that the Group's selling prices were constrained by lower consumer spending and did not kept pace with rising costs. Although Table 8.1 is useful because it shows the figures that underpin the ratios, the line graph shown in Figure 8.3 allows us to see the trend at a glance.

Table 8.1 Ten-year analysis of Ted Baker's operating profit margin

Year	Operating profit/Revenue	Ratio
2005	$\dfrac{£16,405k}{£105,753k} \times 100$	15.51%
2006	$\dfrac{£18,334k}{£117,832k} \times 100$	15.56%
2007	$\dfrac{£20,049k \times 100}{£125,648k}$	15.96%
2008	$\dfrac{£22,142k}{£142,231k} \times 100$	15.57%
2009*	$\dfrac{£17,161k}{£152,661k} \times 100$	11.24%
2010	$\dfrac{£19,782k}{£163,586k} \times 100$	12.09%
2011	$\dfrac{£24,132k}{£187,700k} \times 100$	12.86%
2012*	$\dfrac{£24,269k}{£215,625k} \times 100$	11.26%
2013	$\dfrac{£29,514k}{£254,466k} \times 100$	11.60%
2014	$\dfrac{£39,588k}{£321,921k} \times 100$	12.30%

*Note to readers: While the drop in net profit in 2009 was due to the downturn in the economy, the drop in 2012 was due to reinvesting in the company's future.

Source: Data from Ted Baker PLC financial reports, various years.

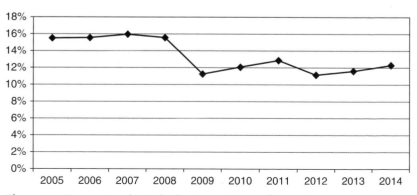

Figure 8.3 Ten-year trend in Ted Baker's operating profit margin

8.8 LIMITATIONS OF RATIO ANALYSIS

All accounting techniques have weaknesses that need to be considered. We can summarise the general *limitations* of ratio analysis as follows:

- Apart from EPS, there are no agreed definitions of the terms used, so ratios based on different definitions will not be comparable. Therefore, it is very important that you define any ambiguous terms and show your formulae when presenting your ratio analysis.
- The figures needed to calculate the ratios may not be disclosed and less precise alternatives may have to be used.
- Comparative data may not be available for previous periods (for example, trend analysis is not possible for a new business).
- Comparative data may not be available for competitors (for example, industry benchmarks may not be available or the business may occupy a niche market).
- Care must be taken when comparing ratios with those of competitors as they may have adopted different accounting policies in respect of deprecation of PPE or valuation of inventory for example.
- Figures in financial statements can be misleading if there is high inflation or unscrupulous manipulation. However, if an unusual accounting treatment has been used, the figures for earlier years are adjusted in published trends.

Any discussion of the limitations of ratio analysis would be incomplete without linking them to the limitations of financial statements:

- Financial statements only contain quantitative data. Therefore, ratio analysis does not take account of non-financial factors such as whether the business has sound plans for the future, a good reputation, a strong customer base, reliable suppliers, loyal employees, obsolete assets, strong competitors, poor industrial relations or activities in a high risk industry.
- Financial statements do not focus on any non-financial effects of transactions or events.
- They do not reflect future transactions or events that may enhance or impair the entity's operations.
- They do not anticipate the impact of potential changes in the economic environment
- There is a substantial degree of classification and aggregation in the financial statements and the effect of allocating continuous operations to the reporting period (ASB, 1999).

Despite these drawbacks, ratio analysis is an invaluable tool for appraising general purpose financial statements. Although ratios do not provide complete answers, they give users an indication of where further investigation may lead to a better understanding of the present and future financial performance and stability of the business.

8.9 KEY POINTS

Ratio analysis is a technique for analysing financial statements that is widely used by investors, lenders, creditors and others to evaluate the financial performance and stability of the business. There are four main types:

- Investment ratios are used to evaluate shareholders' return.
- Profitability ratios are used to assess the operating performance of the business.
- Liquidity and efficiency ratios are used to evaluate the solvency, financial stability and management of working capital of the business.
- Gearing ratios are used to examine the financial structure and assess financial risk.

Despite some limitations, ratio analysis provides additional information that helps users make their different economic decisions. In order to interpret ratios effectively, there needs to be some basis of comparison. Prior year figures are provided in the annual report and accounts, but it is always useful to compare the ratios for competitors or industry benchmarks if data are available. Trend analysis is also useful. Ultimately the choice of analysis depends on the needs of the user and the availability of data.

REVISION QUESTIONS

1. Explain the purpose of ratio analysis. In addition, describe the specific purpose of each of the four main types of ratio.
2. The following extracts are taken from the financial statements of Marsh Ltd and Mallow Ltd.

	Marsh Ltd	Mallow Ltd
	£	£
Capital employed	281,000	596,000
Operating profit	29,500	41,500
Gross profit	71,400	156,200
Revenue	354,900	706,260

Required

(a) Calculate the main profitability ratios for both companies.

(b) Suggest reasons for any differences you find.

3. The following information is taken from Ted Baker's Report and Accounts 2012.

Group Income Statement

For the 52 weeks ended 28 January 2012	Note	2012	2011
		£'000	£'000
Revenue	2	215,625	187,700
Cost of sales		(83,419)	(71,923)
Gross profit		**132,206**	**115,777**
Distribution costs		(82,358)	(73,690)
Administrative expenses		(29,640)	(24,259)
Exceptional costs		(2,814)	–
Licence income		6,733	6,227
Other operating income		142	77
Operating profit		**24,269**	**24,132**
Finance income	4	45	42
Finance expenses	4	(208)	(120)
Share of profit of jointly controlled entity, net of tax	12	149	174
Profit before tax	3,6	**24,255**	**24,228**
Income tax expense	6	(6,698)	(6,948)
Profit for the period		**17,557**	**17,280**

Group Statement of Comprehensive Income

For the 52 weeks ended 28 January 2012	Note	2012	2011
		£'000	£'000
Profit for the period		**17,557**	**17,280**

(Continued)

Other comprehensive income

Net effective portion of changes in fair value of cash flow hedges	(190)	143
Net change in fair value of cash flow hedges transferred to profit or loss	26	(279)
Exchange rate movement	(92)	112
Other comprehensive income for the period	(256)	(24)
Total comprehensive income for the period	**17,301**	**17,256**
Total comprehensive income attributable to:		
– Equity shareholders of the parent company	17,301	17,256
– Non-controlling interest	–	–
Total comprehensive income for the period	**17,301**	**17,256**

Group Balance Sheet

At 28 January 2012	Note	2012	2011
Non-current assets		£'000	£'000
Intangible assets	10	968	997
Property, plant and equipment	11	35,680	28,368
Investment in equity accounted investee	12	494	345
Deferred tax assets	13	3,418	2,470
Prepayments		695	777
		41,255	**32,957**
Current assets			
Inventories	14	51,872	42,492
Trade and other receivables	15	30,587	27,384
Amount due from equity accounted investee	12	407	286
Derivative financial assets	16	411	102
Cash and cash equivalents	17	8,560	13,536
		91,837	**83,800**

(Continued)

		2012	2011
Current liabilities			
Trade and other payables	18	(35,281)	(34,970)
Bank overdraft	17	(6,790)	
Income tax payable		(3,353)	(3,761)
Derivative financial liabilities	16	(1,063)	(455)
		(46,487)	**(39,186)**
Non-current liabilities			
Deferred tax liabilities	13	(1,420)	(1,547)
		(1,420)	**(1,547)**
Net assets		**85,185**	**76,024**
Equity			
Share capital	19	2,160	2,160
Share premium account	19	9,137	9,137
Other reserves	19	(312)	(148)
Translation reserve	19	144	236
Retained earnings	19	74,056	64,639
Total equity attributable to the equity shareholders of the parent company		**85,185**	**76,024**
Non-controlling interest			
Total equity		**85,185**	**76,024**

Extracts from the notes		**2012**	**2011**
4	Of which, interest payable	(208)	(65)
8	Total dividends for the period (£'000)	9,744	8,574
9	Weighted number of ordinary shares ('000)	43,209	41,786
15	Of which, trade receivables (£'000)	19,744	18,182
18	Of which, trade payables (£'000)	(15,910)	(18,888)
20	Weighted average share price (pence)	478.0	441.4
20	Maximum risk free interest rate (%)	4.70	5.29

Required

(a) Calculate the following ratios for 2012 and 2011. Show the formulae (define any ambiguous terms) and all your workings. In each case, explain the purpose of the ratio and interpret your results from an investor's perspective.

  (i) Dividend per share.
  (ii) Dividend yield.
  (iii) Earnings per share.
  (iv) Price-earnings.
  (v) Return on equity.
  (vi) Return on capital employed.
  (vii) Operating profit margin.
  (viii) Capital turnover.

(b) Conclude your analysis with brief comments on any change in the risks and rewards to investors over the period.

4. This question is also based on Ted Baker's Report and Accounts 2012.

Required

(a) Calculate the following ratios for 2012 and 2011. Show the formulae (define any ambiguous terms) and all your workings. In each case, explain the purpose of the ratio and interpret your results from a lender's perspective.

  (i) Current ratio.
  (ii) Acid test.
  (iii) Inventory holding period.
  (iv) Trade receivables collection period.
  (v) Trade payables payment period.
  (vi) Debt/equity.
  (vii) Interest cover.

(b) Conclude your analysis with brief comments on any change in the risks to lenders over the period.

5. Write an essay that discusses the strengths and weaknesses of ratio analysis as a technique for helping users such as investors, lenders and creditors make decisions about providing resources to a business.

REFERENCES

ASB (1999) *Statement of Principles for Financial Reporting*, December, London: Accounting Standards Board.

BIS (2014a) *Business Population Estimates for the UK and Regions 2014*. Available at: www.bis.gov.uk/analysis/statistics/business-population-estimates (Accessed: 12 March 2015).

BIS (2014b) *Statistical Release*, URN14/92, 26 November. Available at: www.bis.gov.uk/analysis/statistics/business-population-estimates (Accessed: 1 December 2014).

BIS (2014c) *Consultation on the UK Implementation of the EU Accounting Directive: Chapters 1–9*. Available at: www.gov.uk/government/consultations/eu-accounting-directive-smaller-companies-reporting (Accessed: 1 December 2014).

Collis, J. (2008) *Directors' Views on Accounting and Auditing Requirements for SMEs*, London: BERR. Available from: http://webarchive.nationalarchives.gov.uk/20090609003228/http:/www.berr.gov.uk/files/file50491.pdf (Accessed 12 March 2015).

Collis, J., Holt, A. and Hussey, R. (2012) *Business Accounting*, 2nd edn, Basingstoke: Palgrave Macmillan.

FRC (2014) *Key Facts and Trends in the Accountancy Profession*, June. Available at: www.frc.org.uk/News-and-Events/FRC-Press/Press/2014/June/FRC-issues-Key-Facts-and-Trends-in-the-Accountancy.aspx (Accessed: 12 March 2015).

Gray, R., Owen, D. and Maunders, K. (1987) *Corporate Social Reporting: Accounting and Accountability*, Harlow: Prentice Hall.

IASB (2003a) IAS 2, *Inventories*, London: International Accounting Standards Board.

IASB (2003b) IAS 33, *Earnings per share*, London: International Accounting Standards Board.

IASB (2008) IAS 16, *Property, Plant and Equipment*, London: International Accounting Standards Board.

IASB (2009a) IFRS 36, *Impairment of Assets*, London: International Accounting Standards Board.

IASB (2009b) *IFRS for SMEs*, London: International Accounting Standards Board.

IASB (2010a) *Conceptual Framework for Financial Reporting*, September, London: International Accounting Standards Board.

IASB (2010b) IFRS 3, *Business Combinations*, London: International Accounting Standards Board.

IASB (2011a) IAS 1, *Presentation of Financial Statements*, London: International Accounting Standards Board.

IASB (2011b) IFRS 10, *Consolidated Financial Statements*, London: International Accounting Standards Board.

IASB (2011c) IFRS 13, *Fair Value Measurement*, London: International Accounting Standards Board.

IASB (2012) IAS 7, *Statement of Cash Flows*, London: International Accounting Standards Board.

IESBA (2013) *Code of Ethics for Professional Accountants*, New York: International Ethics Standards Board for Accountants.

Available at: www.ifac.org/sites/default/files/publications/files/2010-handbook-of-the-code-o.pdf (Accessed: 12 March 2015).

Law, J. (ed) (2010) *Dictionary of Accounting*, 4th edn, Oxford: Oxford University Press.

SBS (2004) *Annual Small Business Survey 2003*, URN 04/390, London: Small Business Service.

Waite, M. (2012) *Paperback Oxford English Dictionary*, Oxford: Oxford University Press.

ANSWERS TO REVISION QUESTIONS

Questions requiring a quantitative answer should be set out clearly. Workings should be shown separately. Some questions require a short narrative answer, a brief report or an essay. The language should be formal and all narrative answers should be written in sentences and paragraphs. Where appropriate, the Harvard system of referencing should be used to support assertions. The model answers provided here are taken from the relevant chapters, but students are encouraged to read more widely.

CHAPTER 1 INTRODUCTION TO FINANCIAL ACCOUNTING

1. Describe how a student can become a qualified professional accountant and explain the need for a code of ethics for professional accountants.

A student wanting to become a professional accountant in the UK must pass a number of rigorous examinations set by one of the recognised accountancy bodies. He or she must then pay an annual subscription to become a member of that body. A qualified accountant can set up in practice as a sole practitioner or with partners, or seek employment in an existing practice. Alternatively, he or she may work as an accountant in the private, public or voluntary sectors.

Professional accountants have a duty to serve the public interest because they are involved in the preparation and auditing of published financial information. They are guided in their work by a code of ethics, which requires them to comply with five fundamental principles (IESBA, 2013, para 100.5):

(a) Integrity – to be straightforward and honest in all professional and business relationships.

(b) Objectivity – to not allow bias, conflict of interest or undue influence of others to override professional judgments.

(c) Professional Competence and Due Care – to maintain professional knowledge and skill at the level required to ensure that a client or employer receives competent professional services based on current developments in practice, legislation and techniques and act diligently and in accordance with applicable technical and professional standards.

(d) Confidentiality – to respect the confidentiality of information acquired as a result of professional and business relationships, and, therefore, not disclose any such information to third parties without proper and specific authority, unless there is a legal or professional right or duty to disclose, nor use the information for the personal advantage of the professional accountant or third parties.

(e) Professional Behavior – to comply with relevant laws and regulations and to avoid any action that discredits the profession.

2. Describe the key elements of the definition of accounting.

In its broadest sense, accounting can be defined as a service provided to those who need financial information. Law (2010, p. 6) is more specific and defines accounting as 'the process of identifying, measuring, recording and communicating economic transactions'.

When identifying the economic transactions, it is important to select the transactions of the business only. This first stage leads to the classification of the transactions into categories, such as purchases, sales revenue and salaries. The economic transactions of the business are measured in monetary terms. This conventional measure is convenient and makes it easier to aggregate, summarise and compare transactions. The transactions are usually recorded in ledger accounts, which are often part of a computerised accounting system, which in turn may be part of an enterprise resource planning system. Communicating economic transactions is achieved by generating a variety of financial statements from the records in the accounting system. These are presented in a format that summarises a particular financial aspect of the business.

3. Compare and contrast the two main branches of accounting.

The two main branches of accounting are financial accounting and management accounting. The purpose of financial accounting is to provide financial information to meet the needs of external users (those not involved in managing the business). On the other hand, the purpose of management accounting is to provide managers with financial and other quantitative information to help them carry out their responsibilities for planning, controlling and decision making. The emphasis is on providing information to internal users that will help the business achieve its financial objectives. Unlike financial accounting, management accounting is not governed by regulations.

Financial accounting is concerned with classifying, measuring and recording the economic transactions of an entity in accordance with established principles, legal requirements and accounting standards. It is primarily concerned with communicating a true and fair view of the financial performance and financial position of an entity to external parties at the end of the accounting period.

On the other hand, management accounting is concerned with collecting and analysing financial and other quantitative information. It is primarily concerned with communicating information to management to help effective performance measurement, planning, controlling and decision making. Therefore, the main differences between the two branches of accounting are that financial accounting is guided by a regulatory framework and focuses on meeting the needs of external users (those not involved in managing the business), and management accounting is unregulated and focuses on meeting the needs of internal users. However, both branches of accounting draw on the same data sources to generate financial information.

4. Explain the advantages and disadvantages of a setting up a one person business as a private limited company rather than a sole proprietorship.

What sole proprietorships and a one person private limited company have in common is that there is only one owner. Unless the owner employs a manager, there is no one with whom to share the responsibility for managing the business and the range of skills available is limited. Both types of business must keep accounting records: the sole proprietorship for taxation purposes only and the private company for taxation and financial reporting purposes.

However, there are some differences. The unincorporated status of a sole proprietorship means there are no formalities involved in setting up the business and the owner has unlimited liability for any debts or losses incurred by the business. On the other hand, a private company is set up through the formal process of incorporation and thus acquires a legal status that is separate from that of its owner. This gives the owner limited liability for any debts or losses incurred by the company. A further distinction is that the name of a private company must end with 'Limited' or 'Ltd' (or the Welsh equivalent) and shares in the company cannot be offered for sale publicly. Finally, a sole proprietorship has no need to make any financial information public, whereas a private company must publish an annual report and accounts within 9 months of the accounting year end. These disclosures must comply with the Companies Act and accounting standards.

5. Discuss the main differences between a public limited company and a private limited company in the UK, paying particular attention to the financial implications.

Limited companies can be divided into private companies and public companies. A private company is any company that is not a public company. A public company is a company limited by shares or limited by guarantee and having share capital. Most companies are started as a private limited company and, if they are successful and grow large, their owners may decide to re-register them as public companies. They can then obtain a listing on a stock exchange and make an initial public offering (IPO). This allows public companies to raise large amounts of capital to fund their activities. However, it is an offence for a private limited company to offer its shares to the public.

There are two main differences between a private company and a public company. First, a public company must state in its memorandum of association that it is a public company and its name must end with the words 'Public Limited Company' or 'PLC' (or the Welsh equivalent). On the other hand, a private company's name must end with the word 'Limited' or the abbreviation 'Ltd' (or the Welsh equivalent). Second, a public company can advertise its shares for sale to the public and, if it has a listing on a stock exchange, its shares can be traded in the stock market. However, a private limited company's shares can only be offered for sale privately.

CHAPTER 2 THE ACCOUNTING SYSTEM

1. Green Landscaping Ltd

Capital account

		£			£
			1 June	Bank	50,000

Bank account

		£			£
1 June	Capital	50,000	1 June	Lorry	16,000
			1 June	Lorry insurance	1,400
			1 June	Rent	4,500
			2 June	Equipment	5,400
			2 June	Purchases	850
			2 June	Advertising	420

Vehicles account

		£		£
1 June	Bank	16,000		

Vehicles insurance account

		£		£
1 June	Bank	1,400		

Rent account

		£		£
1 June	Bank	4,500		

Equipment account

		£		£
1 June	Bank	5,400		

Purchases account

		£		£
2 June	Bank	850		
4 June	Timber supplies	120		

Advertising account

		£		£
2 June	Bank	420		

Timber Supplies Ltd account

	£			£
		4 June	Purchases	120

2. Inspirational Ideas

Sales account

		£			£
			2 July	Cash	138
			3 July	Cash	192

Postage account

		£			£
1 July	Cash	25			
2 July	Cash	31			

Window cleaning account

		£			£
1 July	Cash	10			

Stationery account

		£			£
1 July	Cash	15			
1 July	Cash	36			

Parking account

		£			£
1 July	Cash	2			
2 July	Cash	2			
3 July	Cash	2			

Petrol account

		£			£
1 July	Cash	18			
2 July	Cash	18			

Purchases account

		£			£
2 July	Cash	104			
3 July	Cash	89			

3. Bristol Books Ltd

Bank account

		£			£
1 October	Balance b/f	6,400	2 October	Purchases	750
12 October	Sales	1,800	3 October	Advertising	1,120
15 October	Jones Ltd	950	16 October	Purchases	2,300
18 October	Jones Ltd	950	18 October	Davies Ltd	780
30 October	Sales	1,450	25 October	Purchases	3,400
			31 October	Balance c/f	3,200
		11,550			11,550
1 November	Balance b/f	3,200			

4. Good Food Shop

Good Food Shop Trial balance as at 30 June 2015		
	Debit	Credit
	£	£
Revenue		26,200
Purchases	36,770	
Returns inward	900	
Returns outward		460
Discounts allowed	720	
Discounts received		620

(Continued)

Equipment	2,000	
Bank	1,500	
Salaries	1,600	
Rent	1,400	
General expenses	390	
Capital at 1 July 2014		18,000
	45,280	45,280

5. Explain the advantages of a double-entry bookkeeping system and the purpose of a trial balance. In addition, discuss the limitations of a trial balance, giving examples to illustrate your answer.

Double-entry bookkeeping is 'a method of recording the transactions of a business in a set of accounts, such that every transaction has a dual aspect and therefore needs to be recorded in at least two accounts' (Law, 2010, p. 158). The advantage of recording each transaction at least twice in the accounting system is that it provides an arithmetical check on the accuracy of the records. It is also the most efficient and effective method for recording financial transactions in a way that allows financial statements to be prepared easily.

The purpose of a trial balance is to list the balances on all the accounts at the end of the accounting period, with the debit balances in one column and credit balances in the other. 'If the rules of double-entry bookkeeping have been accurately applied, the totals of each column should be the same' (Law, 2010, p. 420). If they do not balance, checks must be made to identify the reasons for any discrepancies.

The main limitations of a trial balance are that it does not show a number of potential errors. For example, it cannot show transactions that the bookkeeper has failed to record in the accounting system. Nor can it show any transaction that was recorded in the wrong account (for example, in an expense account instead of an asset account). Furthermore, it cannot indicate that the wrong amount was entered (perhaps because the number was transposed – for example, £240 instead of £420), even though the transaction was recorded in the correct accounts. Finally, the trial balance cannot show errors where the transaction was recorded in the correct accounts, but on the wrong side of both accounts. It is important that the accuracy of the trial balance is checked, because the figures form the basis of the financial statements that summarise the transactions that have taken place during the financial period.

CHAPTER 3 FINANCIAL REPORTING FRAMEWORKS

1. Describe the two underlying assumptions that underpin financial accounting and reporting, providing examples to illustrate your answer.

Financial accounting is primarily concerned with communicating a true and fair view of the financial performance and financial position of an entity to external parties at the end of the accounting period. It is underpinned by two fundamental accounting principles: the going concern concept and the accruals concept.

The going concern concept is based on the principle that the business is going to continue in operation for the foreseeable future. Therefore, unless it is known otherwise, it is assumed that the entity is not intending to close down or significantly reduce its activities (IASB, 2010). If that presumption is not valid, the financial statements will need to show the assets of the business at their break-up value (and any liabilities that are applicable on liquidation). For example, equipment would be shown at the estimated market value. IAS 1, *Presentation of Financial Statements* (IASB, 2011) requires management to look at least 12 months ahead to assess whether the entity is a going concern. If there is significant doubt over the entity's ability to continue as a going concern, those uncertainties must be disclosed, together with the basis used.

The accruals concept is the accounting principle that revenue and costs are recognised as they are earned and incurred, not as cash is received or paid (the realisation concept), and they are matched with one another (the matching concept) and dealt with in the income statement of the period to which they relate (the period concept). For example, revenue is matched to the cost of goods sold during the period even if cash has not yet changed hands for either transaction.

2. Describe the three key elements of the regulatory framework for financial reporting. In addition, explain how UK GAAP for listed and unlisted companies is now based on IFRSs.

'Financial reporting refers to the statutory disclosure of general purpose financial information by limited liability entities via the annual report and accounts' (Collis, Holt and Hussey, 2012, p. 16). The key elements of the regulatory framework in the UK are:

- Company law as represented by the Companies Act 2006 (CA2006) and subsequent statutory instruments, which is developed by the government and sanctioned by Parliament.

- National and international accounting standards issued by independent (non-government) bodies, the Financial Reporting Council (FRC) and the International Accounting Standards Board (IASB) respectively.
- Stock exchange rules, which are issued by an independent regulator, the Financial Conduct Authority (FCA).

For many years, the UK issued its own individual financial reporting standards, but today UK GAAP is based on EU-adopted IFRSs:

- FRS 100, *Application of Financial Reporting Requirements* (2012) determines which reporting framework applies to which entities. Listed group entities have been required to use IFRSs since 2005.
- FRS 101, *Reduced Disclosure Framework* (2012) allows subsidiaries in a listed group to use IFRSs, but with fewer disclosures.
- FRS 102, *The Financial Reporting Standard Applicable in the UK and Republic of Ireland* (2013) is based on the IFRS for SMEs. It is a single standard that replaces all previously used UK accounting standards and is applicable to the remaining population of large, medium and small companies.
- FRS 105, *The Financial Reporting Standard applicable to the Micro-Entities Regime* applies to micro-entities from 1 January 2016. It replaces the *Financial Reporting Standard for Smaller Entities (FRSSE)*, which had been a choice for small companies since 1997.

By requiring the use of accounting standards based on IFRS, the UK has helped reduce international differences in financial accounting and reporting practices.

3. Explain what an accounting standard is and discuss the need for international convergence in financial reporting practices.

An accounting standard is 'an authoritative statement on how a particular type of transaction or other event should be reflected in the financial statements. In the UK, compliance with accounting standards is normally necessary for the financial statements to give a true and fair view' (Collis, Holt and Hussey, 2012, p. 99). Accounting standards provide a guide for preparers and auditors of financial statements, but they present a challenge for standard setters, who must decide which accounting methods are appropriate for all companies in all industries and in all circumstances.

Not surprisingly, there are differences in the way countries have developed their regulatory frameworks for financial reporting due to social, economic, legal and cultural reasons. This has resulted in significant differences in accounting practices. For example, some countries in the developing world have minimal financial reporting regulations, while other countries, such as the USA, have highly developed and prescriptive systems.

International differences in accounting standards mean that a company can show one figure of profit when the financial statements are drawn up under one country's rules and a completely different figure when drawn up under another country's rules. These differences are important when a company is seeking a listing on a stock exchange in another country. For example, if a UK company wanted its shares to be traded on the New York Stock Exchange as well as on the London Stock Exchange, it would need to prepare two sets of accounts. This is confusing for users and costly for the company, which must prepare two sets of accounts: once complying with US GAAP and another complying with UK GAAP.

Many businesses now have international operations thanks to the cross-border integration of markets and politics, and this has led to a demand for a single set of global accounting standards. This need has been addressed by the IFRS Foundation, which is the independent, not-for-profit private sector organisation responsible for developing International Financial Reporting Standards (IFRSs) through its standard-setting body, the International Accounting Standards Board (IASB). More than 120 countries require or permit the use of IFRS for some or all of their domestic listed companies and this has helped bring about convergence by reducing international differences in accounting practices.

4. Describe the objective of general purpose financial reporting and discuss the information needs of the three primary user groups identified in the IASB Framework (2010).

According to the IASB Framework (2010), the objective of general purpose financial reporting is to provide information about the reporting entity that is useful to existing and potential investors, lenders and other creditors in making decisions about providing resources to the entity. Those decisions involve buying, selling or holding equity and debt instruments and providing or settling loans and other forms of credit. This principle forms the foundation of the Framework and other aspects of the Framework flow logically from it.

Existing and potential investors need financial information to help them make investment decisions such as buying, selling or holding equity and debt instruments. These decisions depend on the investment risks and returns. Returns might include dividends payable on shares, principal and interest payments or market price increases in equity and debt instruments.

Existing and potential lenders need financial information to help them make lending decisions. These decisions depend on the lending risks and returns. They need to assess whether loans can be repaid and whether the interest they expect to receive will be paid when it is due. As expectations depend on their assessment of the amount, timing and uncertainty of payments, they need information that will help them assess the prospects for future net cash inflows to an entity.

Existing and potential creditors need financial information to help them make credit decisions. These decisions will depend on the credit risks and returns. The latter usually take the form of interest payments. As in the case of lenders, their expectations depend on their assessment of the amount, timing and uncertainty of receiving the amounts owed to them and therefore they need information that will help them assess the prospects for future net cash inflows to an entity.

Investors, lenders and other creditors have a common interest in information about the entity's economic resources and the claims against the reporting entity. This information is shown in the *statement of financial position* (also known as the balance sheet). They are also interested in information about the effects of transactions and other events that change a reporting entity's economic resources and claims). This is shown in the *statement of comprehensive income* (also known as the profit and loss account). Finally, they have a common interest in the changes in the entity's cash flows, which are presented in the *statement of cash flows*. However, one point of difference is that, while lenders and major suppliers have the economic power to demand special purpose financial statements, investors have no such power and must rely on general purpose financial statements.

The Framework acknowledges that general purpose financial reports cannot meet all the information needs of the primary users, many of whom are not in a position to demand special purpose financial reports. Therefore, they will also need to obtain information from other sources such as reports on general economic conditions and expectations, political events and political climate, and industry and company outlooks.

5. Discuss the qualitative characteristics of useful financial information.

The IASB Framework (IASB, 2010) identifies the qualitative characteristics of useful financial information by dividing them into fundamental and enhancing characteristics of usefulness. These accounting principles apply to financial information provided in financial statements, as well as to financial information provided in other ways.

The fundamental qualitative characteristics are:

- *Relevance* – Relevant financial information is capable of making a difference to users' decisions. Financial information is capable of making a difference to decisions if it has predictive value and/or confirmatory value. These two are interrelated. *Materiality* is an entity-specific aspect of relevance based on the nature or magnitude (or both) of the items to which the information relates in the context of an individual entity's financial report. The *materiality concept* is the principle that only items of information that are material (significant) are included in the financial statements. An item of information is material if its omission or misstatement could influence the economic decisions of those using the financial statements. Materiality depends on the size of the item or error and the circumstances of its omission or misstatement (for example, an omission of revenue of £10 versus an omission of £10,000).

- *Faithful representation* – General purpose financial reports represent economic phenomena in words as well as numbers. To be useful, the information must not only represent relevant phenomena but it must also be a faithful representation of the phenomena. Ideally it should be complete, neutral and free from error. Free from error does not mean perfectly accurate. For example, an estimate of an unobservable value cannot be perfectly accurate, but it is a faithful representation if it is clearly described as being an estimate and the nature and limitations of the estimating process are explained, and no errors have been made in selecting and applying an appropriate process for developing the estimate.

Subject to the effects of enhancing characteristics and the cost constraint, the Framework suggests that the most efficient and effective process for applying the fundamental qualitative characteristics would usually be:

1. Identify an economic phenomenon that has the potential to be useful to users of the reporting entity's financial information.
2. Identify the type of information about that phenomenon that would be most relevant if it is available and can be faithfully represented.
3. Determine whether that information is available and can be faithfully represented. If so, the process of satisfying the fundamental qualitative characteristics ends at that point. If not, the process is repeated with the next most relevant type of information.

The Framework points out that the enhancing qualitative characteristics cannot make information useful if that information is irrelevant or it is not faithfully represented. The enhancing qualitative characteristics are:

- *Comparability* – The information is more useful if it can be compared with similar information for the entity in other periods, or similar information for other entities. A comparison requires at least two items. Consistency helps achieve comparability and refers to the use of the same methods for the same items, either from period to period within a reporting entity or in a single period across entities.
- *Verifiability* – The financial information is more useful if it is verifiable. Verifiability helps to assure users that the information is a faithful representation. It means that different knowledgeable and independent observers could reach consensus, although not necessarily complete agreement, that a particular depiction is a faithful representation.
- *Timeliness* – The financial information is more useful if it is timely. Timeliness means that information is available to users in time to be capable of influencing their decisions.
- *Understandability* – The financial information is more useful if it is readily understandable. Classifying, characterising and presenting information clearly and concisely makes it understandable. While some phenomena are inherently complex and cannot be made easy to understand, to exclude such information would make financial reports incomplete and potentially misleading. Financial reports are prepared for users who have a reasonable knowledge of business and economic activities and who review and analyse the information with diligence.

CHAPTER 4 STATEMENT OF COMPREHENSIVE INCOME

1. Describe the general purpose of the statement of comprehensive income. In addition, explain the terms *income* and *expenses* as defined by the Conceptual Framework for Financial Reporting (IASB, 2010).

The purpose of the statement of comprehensive income is to provide information to users on the financial performance of business over the accounting period. Financial performance is concerned with the profitability of the entity. Users need information on the entity's financial performance to assess potential changes in its economic resources and its capacity to generate cash from its resources. In addition, users need information to evaluate how effectively any additional resources might be used. There are two elements of financial performance (IASB, 2010, para 4.25):

- Income is increases in economic benefits during the accounting period in the form of inflows or enhancements of assets or decreases of liabilities that result in increases in equity, other than those relating to contributions from equity participants.
- Expenses are decreases in economic benefits during the accounting period in the form of outflows or depletions of assets or incurrences of liabilities that result in decreases in equity, other than those relating to distributions to equity participants.

2. Explain the accrual basis of accounting by defining the principles involved. Illustrate your answer by taking the example of the cost of sales adjustment in the statement of comprehensive income.

Apart from cash flow information, financial statements are prepared using the accrual basis of accounting. The accruals concept is the principle that revenue and costs are recognised as they are earned and incurred not as cash is received or paid (the realisation concept), and they are matched with one another (the matching concept) and dealt with in the income statement of the period to which they relate (the time period concept). Under the accrual basis of accounting, the effects of economic transactions and events are shown in the period in which they occur, even if the resulting cash receipts and payments occur in a different period. In cash accounting, transactions and events are only recognised when cash has been received or paid.

For example, during the month of January a car dealer sold a vehicle for £7,500 that he had purchased at the beginning of the month for £5,000. Both transactions were on credit and at the end of the month no cash had changed hands. Using the accruals concept, the revenue and cost of sales are matched to each other and to the accounting period. Therefore, the profit is calculated as revenue (£7,500) minus cost of sales (£5,000) = £2,500.

3. Uptown Ltd

Uptown Ltd Statement of comprehensive income for the year ended 31 December 2015	
	£
Revenue	66,500
Cost of sales (W1)	(12,000)
Gross profit	54,500

(Continued)

Bank interest received	100
Rent and rates	(24,000)
Salaries	(21,500)
Insurance	(2,000)
Lighting and heating	(500)
Telephone and Internet	(400)
Advertising	(100)
Operating profit	6,100
Income tax expense	(2,000)
Profit for the period	4,100

W1 Cost of sales	£
Purchases	20,000
Closing inventory	(8,000)
	12,000

4. MiGame Ltd

(a)

MiGame Ltd
Draft statement of comprehensive income
for the year ended 30 June 2015

	£
Revenue	75,200
Cost of sales (W1)	(11,270)
Gross profit	63,930
Other income	1,200
Salaries	(24,000)
Rent and rates	(18,000)
Insurance	(7,200)
Advertising (W2)	(600)
Lighting and heating (W2)	(1,160)
Telephone and Internet (W2)	(740)
General expenses	(410)
Operating profit	13,020
Income tax expense	(1,200)
Profit for the period	11,820

W1 Cost of sales	£
Purchases	12,160
Closing inventory	(890)
	11,270

W2 Accruals and prepayments	TB	Accrued	Prepaid	Total
	£	£	£	£
Advertising	860		(260)	600
Lighting and heating	620	540		1,160
Telephone and Internet	450	290		740
General expenses	250	160		410

(b)

MiGame Ltd Statement of comprehensive income for the year ended 30 June 2015	
	£
Revenue	75,200
Cost of sales (W1)	(11,270)
Gross profit	63,930
Rental income	1,200
Salaries	(24,000)
Rent and rates	(18,000)
Insurance	(7,200)
Advertising (W2)	(600)
Lighting and heating (W2)	(1,160)
Telephone and Internet (W2)	(740)
General expenses	(410)
Allowances:	
Depreciation on plant and equipment (W3)	(5,000)
Doubtful receivables (W4)	(120)
Operating profit	7,900
Income tax expense	(1,200)
Profit for the period	6,700

W1 Cost of sales	£
Purchases	12,160
Closing inventory	(890)
	11,270

W2 Accruals and prepayments	TB	Accrued	Prepaid	Total
	£	£	£	£
Advertising	860		(260)	600
Lighting and heating	620	540		1,160
Telephone and Internet	450	290		740
General expenses	250	160		410

W3 PPE	£
Plant and equipment at cost	25,000
Allowance for depreciation (÷ 5 years)	(5,000)

W4 Trade receivables	£
Trade receivables per TB	1,200
10% Allowance for doubtful receivables	(120)

(c)

MiGame Ltd Statement of comprehensive income for the year ended 30 June 2015	
	£
Revenue	75,200
Cost of sales (W1)	(11,270)
Gross profit	63,930
Rental income	1,200
Distribution costs (W5)	(28,855)

(Continued)

Administrative expenses (W5)	(28,375)
Operating profit	7,900
Income tax expense	(1,200)
Profit for the period	6,700

W1 Cost of sales	£
Purchases	12,160
Closing inventory	(890)
	11,270

W2 Accruals and prepayments	TB	Accrued	Prepaid	Total
	£	£	£	£
Advertising	860		(260)	600
Lighting and heating	620	540		1,160
Telephone and Internet	450	290		740
General expenses	250	160		410

W3 PPE	£
Plant and equipment at cost	25,000
Allowance for depreciation (÷ 5 years)	(5,000)

W4 Trade receivables	£
Trade receivables in trial balance	1,200
10% allowance for doubtful receivables	(120)

W5 Expense analysis	Amount	Distribution costs	Administrative expenses	Finance costs
	£	£	£	£
Salaries	24,000	12,000	12,000	
Rent and rates	18,000	9,000	9,000	
Insurance	7,200	3,600	3,600	

(Continued)

W5 Expense analysis (continued)	Amount	Distribution costs	Administrative expenses	Finance costs
	£	£	£	£
Advertising (W2)	600	600		
Lighting and heating (W2)	1,160	580	580	
Telephone and Internet (W2)	740	370	370	
General expenses	410	205	205	
Allowances:				
Depreciation: Plant and equipment (W3)	5,000	2,500	2,500	
Doubtful receivables (W4)	120		120	
	57,230	28,855	28,375	0

5. Beauty Plus Ltd

Beauty Plus Ltd
Statement of comprehensive income
for the year ended 30 June 2015

	£
Revenue	104,900
Cost of sales (W1)	(37,700)
Gross profit	67,200
Interest received	100
Salaries	(30,000)
Rent and rates	(15,000)
Insurance	(3,000)
Lighting and heating	(1,500)
Telephone and Internet	(2,000)
Advertising	(500)
Allowances:	
Depreciation on equipment (W2)	(4,000)
Doubtful receivables (W3)	400
Operating profit	11,700
Income tax expense	(4,500)
Profit for the period	7,200

W1 Cost of sales	£
Opening inventory	10,000
Purchases	39,700
Closing inventory	(12,000)
	37,700

W2 PPE	£
Equipment at cost	20,000
Allowance for depreciation (÷ 5 years)	(4,000)

W3 Trade receivables	£
Trade receivables per TB	6,000
Year 2 doubtful receivables	(600)
Adjusted trade receivables	5,400
Year 1 doubtful debts	(1,000)
Decrease in doubtful receivables (1,000–600)	400

CHAPTER 5 STATEMENT OF FINANCIAL POSITION

1. Describe the general purpose of the statement of financial position. In addition, explain the terms *asset, liability* and *equity* as defined by the *Conceptual Framework for Financial Reporting* (IASB, 2010).

The purpose of the *statement of financial position* is to summarise the assets, equity and liabilities of the business on the last day of the accounting period for which the statement of comprehensive income was prepared. The statement of financial position reflects the accounting equation: Assets = Equity + Liabilities. These three elements of financial position are defined by the IASB (2010, para 4.25) as follows:

- An asset is a resource controlled by the entity as a result of past events and from which future economic benefits are expected to flow to the entity.
- A liability is a present obligation of the entity resulting from past events, the settlement of which is expected to result in an outflow from the entity of resources embodying economic benefits.
- Equity is the residual interest in the assets of the entity after deducting all its liabilities.

Assets are what the business owns, such as premises, machinery, vehicles, equipment, inventory and cash. Liabilities are what the business owes to others apart from the owners, such as money owed to lenders and suppliers. Equity represents the owners' interest in the business and is what remains once the liabilities are subtracted from the assets.

2. Explain the going concern basis of accounting by defining the principles involved. Illustrate your answer by taking the example of the valuation of tangible assets in the statement of financial position.

The going concern concept is based on the principle that the entity will continue in operation for the foreseeable future. Therefore, unless it is known otherwise, it is assumed that the entity is not intending to close down or significantly reduce its activities. If that presumption is not valid, the financial statements will need to show the assets of the business at their break-up value and any liabilities that are applicable on liquidation (IASB, 2010a). Management must look at least 12 months ahead and, if there is significant doubt over the entity's ability to continue as a going concern, those uncertainties must be disclosed, together with the basis used (IASB, 2011a).

For example, if the business is a going concern, tangible assets with a finite life are shown at the carrying value (cost minus accumulated depreciation). However, if the business is closing down, they are shown at the estimated market value, which may be considerably lower.

3. Uptown Ltd

Uptown Ltd Statement of comprehensive income for the year ended 31 December 2015	
	£
Revenue	66,500
Cost of sales (W1)	(12,000)
Gross profit	54,500
Bank interest received	100
Rent and rates	(24,000)
Salaries	(21,500)

(Continued)

Insurance	(2,000)
Lighting and heating	(500)
Telephone and Internet	(400)
Advertising	(100)
Operating profit	6,100
Income tax expense	(2,000)
Profit for the period	4,100

W1 Cost of sales	£
Purchases	20,000
Closing inventory	(8,000)
	12,000

4. MiGame Ltd

(a)

MiGame Ltd Draft statement of comprehensive income for the year ended 30 June 2015	
	£
Revenue	75,200
Cost of sales (W1)	(11,270)
Gross profit	63,930
Other income	1,200
Salaries	(24,000)
Rent and rates	(18,000)
Insurance	(7,200)
Advertising (W2)	(600)
Lighting and heating (W2)	(1,160)
Telephone and Internet (W2)	(740)
General expenses	(410)
Operating profit	13,020
Income tax expense	(1,200)
Profit for the period	11,820

MiGame Ltd

Draft statement of financial position at 30 June 2015

	£
ASSETS	
Non-current assets	
Property, plant and equipment (at cost)	25,000
Current assets	
Inventory	890
Trade and other receivables (W3)	1,460
Cash and cash equivalents	3,260
	5,610
Total assets	30,610
EQUITY AND LIABILITIES	
Equity	
Share capital	15,000
Retained earnings	11,820
	26,820
Current liabilities	
Trade and other payables (W4)	2,590
Current tax payable	1,200
	3,790
Total equity and liabilities	30,610

W1 Cost of sales	£
Purchases	12,160
Closing inventory	(890)
	11,270

W2 Accruals and prepayments	TB	Accrued	Prepaid	Total
	£	£	£	£
Advertising	860		(260)	600
Lighting and heating	620	540		1,160

(Continued)

W2 Accruals and prepayments	TB	Accrued	Prepaid	Total
Telephone and Internet	450	290		740
General expenses	250	160		410
Total accrued and prepaid		990	(260)	

W3 Trade and other receivables	£
Opening trade receivables	1,200
Prepayments (W2)	260
	1,460

W4 Trade and other payables	£
Opening trade payables	1,600
Accruals (W2)	990
	2,590

(b)

MiGame Ltd Statement of comprehensive income for the year ended 30 June 2015	
	£
Revenue	75,200
Cost of sales (W1)	(11,270)
Gross profit	63,930
Rental income	1,200
Salaries	(24,000)
Rent and rates	(18,000)
Insurance	(7,200)
Advertising (W2)	(600)
Lighting and heating (W2)	(1,160)
Telephone and Internet (W2)	(740)
General expenses	(410)

(Continued)

Allowances:	
Depreciation on plant and equipment (W3)	(5,000)
Doubtful receivables (W4)	(120)
Operating profit	7,900
Income tax expense	(1,200)
Profit for the period	6,700

MiGame Ltd
Statement of financial position at 30 June 2015

	£
ASSETS	
Non-current assets	
Property, plant and equipment (W3)	20,000
Current assets	
Inventory	890
Trade and other receivables (W4)	1,340
Cash and cash equivalents	3,260
	5,490
Total assets	25,490
EQUITY AND LIABILITIES	
Equity	
Share capital	15,000
Retained earnings	6,700
	21,700
Current liabilities	
Trade and other payables (W5)	2,590
Current tax payable	1,200
	3,790
Total equity and liabilities	25,490

W1 Cost of sales	£
Purchases	12,160
Closing inventory	(890)
	11,270

W2 Accruals and prepayments	TB	Accrued	Prepaid	Total
	£	£	£	£
Advertising	860		(260)	600
Lighting and heating	620	540		1,160
Telephone and Internet	450	290		740
General expenses	250	160		410
Total accrued and prepaid		990	(260)	

W3 PPE	£
PPE at cost	25,000
Year 1 depreciation	(5,000)
Closing carrying amount	20,000

W4 Trade and other receivables	£
Trade receivables per TB	1,200
Allowance for doubtful receivables	(120)
Adjusted trade receivables	1,080
Prepayments	260
	1,340

W5 Trade and other payables	£
Trade payables per TB	1,600
Accruals	990
	2,590

(c)

MiGame Ltd
Statement of comprehensive income
for the year ended 30 June 2015

	£
Revenue	75,200
Cost of sales (W1)	(11,270)
Gross profit	63,930

(Continued)

Rental income	1,200
Distribution costs (W6)	(28,855)
Administrative expenses (W6)	(28,375)
Operating profit	7,900
Income tax expense	(1,200)
Profit for the period	6,700

MiGame Ltd
Statement of financial position at 30 June 2015

	£
ASSETS	
Non-current assets	
Property, plant and equipment (W3)	20,000
Current assets	
Inventory	890
Trade and other receivables (W4)	1,340
Cash	3,260
	5,490
Total assets	25,490
EQUITY AND LIABILITIES	
Equity	
Share capital	15,000
Retained earnings	6,700
	21,700
Current liabilities	
Trade and other payables (W5)	2,590
Current tax payable	1,200
	3,790
Total equity and liabilities	25,490

W1 Cost of sales	£
Purchases	12,160
Closing inventory	(890)
11,270

W2 Accruals and prepayments	TB	Accrued	Prepaid	Total
£	£	£	£
Advertising	860		(260)	600
Lighting and heating	620	540		1,160
Telephone and Internet	450	290		740
General expenses	250	160		410
Total accrued and prepaid		990	(260)

W3 PPE	£
PPE at cost	25,000
Year 1 depreciation	(5,000)
Closing carrying amount	20,000

W4 Trade and other receivables	£
Trade receivables per TB	1,200
Allowance for doubtful receivables	(120)
Adjusted trade receivables	1,080
Prepayments	260
1,340

W5 Trade and other payables	£
Trade payables per TB	1,600
Accruals	990
2,590

W6 Expense analysis	Amount	Distribution costs	Administrative expenses	Finance costs
	£	£	£	£
Salaries	24,000	12,000	12,000	
Rent and rates	18,000	9,000	9,000	
Insurance	7,200	3,600	3,600	
Advertising (W2)	600	600		
Lighting and heating (W2)	1,160	580	580	
Telephone and Internet (W2)	740	370	370	
General expenses	410	205	205	
Allowances:				
Depreciation: Plant and equipment (W3)	5,000	2,500	2,500	
Doubtful receivables (W4)	120		120	
	57,230	28,855	28,375	0

5. Beauty Plus Ltd

Beauty Plus Ltd
Statement of comprehensive income
for the year ended 30 June 2016

	£
Revenue	104,900
Cost of sales (W1)	(37,700)
Gross profit	67,200
Interest received	100
Salaries	(30,000)
Rent and rates	(15,000)
Insurance	(3,000)
Lighting and heating	(1,500)
Telephone and Internet	(2,000)
Advertising	(500)

(Continued)

Allowances:	
Depreciation on equipment (W2)	(4,000)
Doubtful receivables (W3)	400
Operating profit	11,700
Income tax expense	(4,500)
Profit for the period	7,200

Beauty Plus Ltd
Statement of financial position at 30 June 2016

	£
ASSETS	
Non-current assets	
Property, plant and equipment (W2)	12,000
Current assets	
Inventory	12,000
Trade and other receivables (W3)	5,400
Cash	15,300
	32,700
Total assets	44,700
EQUITY AND LIABILITIES	
Equity	
Share capital	20,000
Retained earnings	12,200
	32,200
Current liabilities	
Trade and other payables	8,000
Current tax payable	4,500
	12,500
Total equity and liabilities	44,700

W1 Cost of sales	£
Opening inventory	10,000
Purchases	39,700
Closing inventory	(12,000)
	37,700

W2 PPE	Year	Opening carrying amount	Depreciation	Closing carrying amount
		£	£	£
Equipment	1	20,000	(4,000)	16,000
Equipment	2	16,000	(4,000)	12,000

W3 Doubtful receivables	£
Trade receivables in trial balance	6,000
Year 2 doubtful receivables	(600)
Adjusted trade receivables	5,400
Year 1 doubtful receivables	(1,000)
Decrease in doubtful receivables	400

CHAPTER 6 STATEMENT OF CASH FLOWS

1. Explain the purpose of the statement of cash flows and differentiate between cash and cash equivalents.

IAS 7, *Statement of Cash Flows* (IASB, 2012) requires all entities that comply with IFRS to prepare a statement of cash flows, the purpose of which is to provide information about the historical changes in cash and cash equivalents. 'Cash comprises cash on hand and demand deposits' (IAS 7, para 7). Examples of cash on hand are money and cheques held in the business or money at the bank. Examples of demand deposits are money held on short-term deposit at a bank or other financial institution. 'Cash equivalents are short-term, highly liquid investments that are readily convertible to known amounts of cash and which are subject to an insignificant risk of changes in value' (IAS 7, para 7). Examples of cash equivalents are treasury bills, short-term government bonds and money market holdings.

Cash equivalents are held for the purpose of meeting short-term cash commitments rather than for investment or other purposes. An investment normally qualifies as a cash equivalent when it has a short maturity of, say, three months or less from the date of acquisition. Equity investments are excluded from cash equivalents unless they are, in substance, cash equivalents (such as preference shares acquired within a short period of their maturity and with a specified redemption date).

Bank overdrafts are generally classified as borrowings, but IAS 7 notes that if a bank overdraft is repayable on demand and forms an integral part of an entity's cash management, it is included as a component of cash and cash equivalents. A characteristic of such a banking arrangement is that the bank balance often fluctuates from being positive to overdrawn.

2. Explain the difference between operating, investing and financing activities.

IAS 7, *Statement of Cash Flows* (IASB, 2012) requires the information in the statement of cash flows to be classified into cash flows from operating, investing and financing activities. 'Operating activities are the principal revenue generating activities of the entity and other activities that are not investing or financing activities' (IAS 7, para 6). Examples include:

- Cash receipts from customers.
- Cash receipts from other revenue, such as royalties and commissions.
- Cash payments to suppliers.
- Cash payments to and on behalf of employees.
- Cash payments in respect of interest on loans for operating purposes.
- Cash payments of income tax and income tax refunds that relate to operating activities.

These cash flows relate to transactions and events reported in the statement of comprehensive income. The net cash flow from operating activities is an important measure of an entity's ability to generate sufficient cash to replace assets, pay dividends and make new investments without having to use external sources of finance. This information can also be used to forecast future operating cash flows.

'Investing activities are the acquisition and disposal of long-term assets and other investments not included in cash equivalents' (IAS 7, para 6). Examples include:

- Cash receipts from the sale of redundant non-current assets and intangible assets.
- Cash receipts from the sale of equity or debt instruments (such as shares or debentures) of other entities.
- Cash receipts from the repayment of advances and loans made to other parties.
- Cash payments to acquire property, plant and equipment and intangible assets.

- Cash payments to acquire equity and debt instruments (such as shares or debentures) of other entities.
- Cash payments in respect of advances and loans made to other parties.

'Financing activities are activities that result in changes in the size and composition of the contributed equity and borrowings of the entity' (IAS 7, para 6). Examples include:

- Cash receipts from issuing shares.
- Cash receipts from issuing debentures and loans.
- Cash payments to owners to acquire or redeem the entity's shares.
- Cash repayments of amounts borrowed or amounts paid to reduce a liability under a finance lease.

3. Compare and contrast the direct and indirect methods for presenting cash flows for operating activities.

IAS 7, *Statement of Cash Flows* (IASB, 2012) allows the cash flows from operating activities to be reported using the direct method or the indirect method. Both methods result in the same figure for the net cash flows from operating activities.

Under the direct method, each major class of gross cash receipts and gross cash payments from operating activities is shown separately and then aggregated to give the total cash generated from operating activities. Under the indirect method, the starting point is the operating profit, which is then adjusted for the effects of the following transactions which are part of the operating activities of the business:

- Non-cash expenses, such as depreciation, impairment of goodwill and any change in the allowance for doubtful receivables.
- Non-cash income, such as gains on the sale of non-current assets and a decrease in the allowance for doubtful receivables.
- Changes in non-cash working capital items, such as inventory, trade receivables, prepaid expenses, trade payables and accrued expenses.
- Items of income or expense associated with investing or financing cash flows.

The main advantage of the direct method is that it presents the firm's operating cash receipts and payments very clearly. On the other hand, it is more complex than the indirect method and provides more information that could be useful to competitors. The main advantage of the indirect method is that it focuses on the differences between net income and operating cash flow, which provides a useful link to the income statement when forecasting future operating cash flow. It is also easier to calculate than the direct method. However, it can be less understandable to users as the reconciliation of operating profit to cash generated from operations is subject to distortion if the company reclassifies assets from non-current to current assets during the period. Although IAS 7 encourages the use of the direct method because it supplies more relevant information and is more understandable to users, most companies using IAS 7 prefer the indirect method.

4. Beauty Plus Ltd

(a) Direct method

Beauty Plus Ltd Statement of cash flows for year ended 30 June 2016	
	£
Cash flows from operating activities	
Cash receipts from customers (W1)	108,900
Cash paid to suppliers of goods and services (W2)	(57,700)
Cash paid to employees	(30,000)
Cash generated from operations	21,200
Taxation paid	(3,000)
Interest received	100
Net cash inflow from operating activities	18,300
Cash flows from investing activities	
Acquisition of property, plant and equipment	-
Cash flows from financing activities	
Bank loan repaid	(11,000)
Net increase in cash and cash equivalents	7,300
Cash and cash equivalents at 1 July 2015	8,000
Cash and cash equivalents at 30 June 2016	15,300

W1 Cash receipts from customers	£
Revenue	104,900
Opening trade receivables	10,000
Closing trade receivables	(6,000)
	108,900

W2 Cash paid to suppliers of goods and services	£
Purchases of inventory	(39,700)
Opening trade payables	(4,000)
Closing trade payables	8,000
Operating expenses (excluding salaries, depreciation and bad receivables adjustments)	(22,000)
	(57,700)

(b)   Indirect method

Beauty Plus Ltd Statement of cash flows for the year ended 30 June 2016	
	£
Cash flows from operating activities	
Operating profit	11,700
Depreciation	4,000
Increase in inventory	(2,000)
Decrease in trade receivables	3,600
Increase in trade payables	4,000
Interest received	(100)
Cash generated from operations	21,200
Income taxes paid	(3,000)
Interest received	100
Net cash inflows from operating activities	18,300
Cash flows from investing activities	
Acquisition of property, plant and equipment	-
Cash flows from financing activities	
Bank loan repaid	(11,000)
Net increase in cash and cash equivalents	7,300
Cash and cash equivalents at 1 July 2015	8,000
Cash and cash equivalents at 30 June 2016	15,300

(c) Comment on the net increase or decrease in cash and cash equivalents during the year and on whether it was the result of operating, investing or financing activities.

The statement of cash flows for Beauty Plus Ltd shows that there was a net increase of £15,300 in cash and cash equivalents during the financial year. This comprises £8,000 at the start of the period and a net increase of £7,300 during the year. Although Beauty Plus Ltd had no cash flows from investing activities, the company generated £21,200 cash from operating activities during the year and used £11,000 of this to repay the bank loan.

5. Henley Ltd

(a) Direct method

Henley Ltd	
Statement of cash flows for the year ended 31 December 2015	
	£
Cash flows from operating activities	
Cash receipts from customers (W1)	100,000
Cash paid to suppliers of goods and services (W2)	(67,600)
Cash paid to employees	(20,000)
Cash generated from operating activities	12,400
Taxation paid	(3,000)
Interest paid	(1,100)
Net cash inflow from operating activities	8,300
Cash flows from investing activities	
Cash proceeds from sale of non-current assets	12,000
Acquisition of property, plant and equipment	(15,000)
Net cash outflow from investing activities	(3,000)
Cash flows from financing activities	
Dividends paid	(6,000)
Bank loan	5,000
Net cash outflow from financing activities	(1,000)
Net increase in cash and cash equivalents	4,300
Cash and cash equivalents at 1 January 2015	8,000
Cash and cash equivalents at 31 December 2015	12,300

W1 Cash receipts from customers	£
Revenue	120,000
Opening trade receivables	10,000
Closing trade receivables	(30,000)
	100,000

W2 Cash paid to suppliers of goods and services	£
Purchases of inventory	(62,000)
Opening trade payables	(4,000)
Closing trade payables	8,000
Operating expenses (excluding salaries, depreciation, bad receivables and profit on disposal)	(9,600)
	(67,600)

(b) Indirect method

Henley Ltd	
Statement of cash flows for the year ended 31 December 2015	
	£
Cash flows from operating activities	
Profit before tax	28,300
Depreciation	8,000
Profit on disposal of property	(9,000)
Increase in inventory	(2,000)
Increase in net accounts receivable	(18,000)
Increase in trade payables	4,000
Interest paid	1,100
Cash generated from operations	12,400
Taxation paid	(3,000)
Interest paid	(1,100)
Net cash inflow from operating activities	8,300
Cash flows from investing activities	
Cash proceeds from sale of fixed assets	12,000

(Continued)

Acquisition of property, plant and equipment	(15,000)
Net cash outflow from investing activities	(3,000)
Cash flows from financing activities	
Dividends paid	(6,000)
Bank loan	5,000
Net cash outflow from financing activities	(1,000)
Net increase in cash and cash equivalents	4,300
Cash and cash equivalents at 1 January 2015	8,000
Cash and cash equivalents at 31 December 2015	12,300

(c) Review the cash flow position of Henley Ltd at 31 December 2015.

The statement of cash flows shows that at the end of the year the company had cash and cash equivalents of £12,300. This was the result of the company generating net cash inflows of £8,300 from its operating activities, net cash outflows from investing activities of £3,000, net cash outflows of £1,000 from financing activities. The position at the end of the year also takes account of £8,000 in cash and cash equivalents at the start of the year.

CHAPTER 7 CONSOLIDATED FINANCIAL STATEMENTS

1. Explain how to determine whether a transaction is a business combination. In addition, describe the principle of control.

Most large companies in the UK are the result of business combinations. According to IFRS 3, *Business Combinations* (IASB, 2010, Appendix A), a business combination is 'a transaction or other event in which an acquirer obtains control of one or more businesses'. Mergers of equals are also business combinations. Examples of how a business combination can occur include transferring cash, incurring liabilities, issuing equity instruments or by contract alone. The business combination can be structured in various ways, such as one entity becoming a subsidiary of another entity (the parent) or the transfer of net assets from one entity to another entity or to a new entity.

The business combination must involve the acquisition of a business, which generally has three elements:

• Inputs – an economic resource that creates outputs when one or more processes are applied to it (for example non-current assets or intangible assets).

- Process – a system, standard, protocol, convention or rule that when applied to an input or inputs, creates outputs (for example strategic management, operational processes).
- Output – the result of inputs and processes applied to those inputs.

Under IFRS 10, *Consolidated Financial Statements* (IASB, 2011), an investor determines whether it is a parent by assessing whether it controls one or more investees, and the investor must consider all the relevant facts and circumstances when making this assessment. An investor controls an investee when the investor possesses all the following elements of control:

- Power over the investee by having existing rights that give the investor the ability to direct the relevant activities of the investee.
- Exposure to or rights to variable returns from the investor's involvement with the investee.
- The ability of the investor to use its power over the investee to affect the amount of the investor's returns.

In contrast, an investment that offers joint control provides a contractually agreed sharing of control where strategic decisions about the relevant activities, such as capital expenditure and approving a business plan, require the unanimous consent of the parties sharing control.

2. Explain the purpose of the consolidated financial statements and the reason why goodwill is only shown in the consolidated financial statements.

The purpose of consolidated financial statements is to present the assets, liabilities, equity, income, expenses and cash flows of the parent and its subsidiaries as if they were a single economic entity. IFRS 10, *Consolidated Financial Statements* (IASB, 2011) requires a parent to prepare consolidated financial statements for the shareholders of the parent company, who will receive them in addition to the parent's financial statements.

IFRS 3, *Business Combinations* (IASB, 2010b) states that goodwill can only be recognised as a result of a business combination. Goodwill is 'an asset representing the future economic benefits arising from other assets acquired in a business combination that are not individually identified and separately recognised' (IASB, 2010, Appendix A). Examples include the company's reputation, the loyalty of its workforce and its customer base. Under the acquisition method set out in IFRS 3, the consolidated financial statements must recognise and measure goodwill or a gain from a bargain purchase at acquisition-date fair value. Goodwill at the date of acquisition is the excess of the fair value of the consideration transferred, plus the value of any NCI, less the fair value of the identifiable net assets acquired. After acquisition, goodwill is shown in the consolidated statement of financial position at cost, less any accumulated impairment losses. Any impairment loss is written off against the group's retained earnings.

3. Explain why the net assets of a subsidiary should be adjusted to their fair value at the date of acquisition.

Under IFRS 3, *Business Combinations* (IASB, 2010), a business combination is accounted for at acquisition by preparing consolidated financial statements using the acquisition method. IFRS 3 requires that a subsidiary's identifiable assets and liabilities should be recognised at fair value rather than current book value (carrying value) at the date of acquisition. According to IFRS 13, *Fair Value* Measurement (IASB, 2011, Appendix A), fair value is 'the price that would be received to sell an asset or paid to transfer a liability in an orderly transaction between market participants at the measurement date'. The four main bases of fair value are current cost, net realisable value, value in use and replacement cost. IFRS 3 requires measurement of a subsidiary's assets and liabilities at fair value as it provides a faithful representation of their economic value at the date of acquisition.

4. Polymatica PLC

		£'000
	Fair value of consideration transferred	500
(a)	NCI at 1 July 2016 (£300k × 20%)	60
	Fair value of subsidiary's net assets at 1 July 2016	(300)
(b)	Goodwill (balancing figure)	260

5. Brewer Ltd

(a)

	£
Fair value of consideration transferred	60,000
Non-controlling interest (£66,250 × 20%)	13,250
Fair value of identifiable assets at 1 August 2015	(66,250)
Goodwill	7,000

(b)

Consolidated statement of financial position at 31 July 2016							
	Brewer Ltd	Cooper Ltd	W1	W2	W3	W4	Group
	£	£	£	£	£	£	£
ASSETS							
Non-current assets							
Property, plant and equipment	150,000	82,000					232,000
Investment in Cooper Ltd	60,000	–	(60,000)	–	–	–	–
Goodwill	–	–	7,000	–	–	(3,500)	3,500
	210,000	82,000	(53,000)	–	–	(3,500)	235,500
Current assets	195,000	92,250	–	–	–	–	287,250
Total assets	405,000	174,250	(53,000)	–	–	(3,500)	522,750
EQUITY AND LIABILITIES							
Equity							
Ordinary share capital	250,000	50,000	(40,000)	(10,000)	–	–	250,000
Retained earnings pre-acquisition	–	16,250	(13,000)	(3,250)	–	–	–
Retained earnings post acquisition	32,000	20,000	–	–	(4,000)	(3,500)	44,500
Revaluation reserve	–	10,000	–	–	(2,000)	–	8,000
Non-controlling interest	–	–	–	13,250	6,000	–	19,250
	282,000	96,250	(53,000)	–	–	(3,500)	321,750
Current liabilities	123,000	78,000	–	–	–	–	201,000
Total equity and liabilities	405,000	174,250	(53,000)	–	–	(3,500)	522,750

W1 recognises goodwill by deducting the parent's 80% share of Cooper Ltd's identifiable net assets (£60,000).

W2 recognises the NCI by deducting its 20% share of Cooper's identifiable net assets at the acquisition date.

W3 recognises the NCI's 20% share in Cooper Ltd's post acquisition profits of £20,000 (£4,000), in Cooper's post acquisition revaluation reserve of £10,000 (£2,000), and in Cooper's post acquisition profits of £20,000 (£6,000).

W4 accounts for the 50% impairment of goodwill (£3,500).

CHAPTER 8

1. Explain the purpose of ratio analysis. In addition, describe the specific purpose of each of the four main types of ratio.

The purpose of ratio analysis is to evaluate the financial performance and financial stability of a business using accounting ratios. A ratio describes a quantitative relationship between two data items. Any number of ratios can be calculated and the choice depends on the needs of the user and the availability of relevant data. 'In conducting an analysis comparisons will be made with other companies and with industry averages over a period of time. The analysis of ratios can indicate how well a company is run, the risks of financial insolvency, and the financial returns provided' (Law, 2010, p. 345). The results of the analysis provide additional information that helps investors, lenders, creditors and other users of the financial statements make their different economic decisions.

There are four main types of ratio and each has specific purpose:

- *Investment ratios* are used for evaluating shareholders' return. They are widely used by existing and potential investors (and their advisers) to aid their investment decisions.
- *Profitability ratios* are used for assessing the operating performance of the business. They are used by internal and external users to assess how effectively the directors have been in managing the business in terms of generating income and controlling costs. Not only are investors, lenders and creditors interested in the profitability of the business, but also employees, major suppliers and customers.
- *Liquidity and efficiency ratios* are used for evaluating the solvency, financial stability and management of working capital of the business. Liquidity ratios are used to evaluate the solvency and financial stability of a business and are relevant to all users who have an interest in whether the business is a going concern. The liquidity of the business is of particular importance to lenders and creditors who need to assess whether the business is able to service loans and pay for goods and services bought on credit. Efficiency ratios (or funds management ratios) are used to assess how effectively the directors have managed working capital.
- *Gearing ratios* are used for examining the financial structure of the business and assessing financial risk. Gearing (or leverage) refers to the relationship between equity and long-term debt finance in the business. The financial structure of a business can have an impact on its financial performance and gearing ratios are used by investors and lenders to assess financial risk when a business has an obligation to service and repay long-term debt(s).

2. Marsh Ltd and Mallow Ltd

(a) Profitability ratios

	Marsh Ltd	Mallow Ltd
Return on capital employed		
$\dfrac{\text{Operating profit}}{\text{Capital employed}} \times 100$	$\dfrac{£29,500k}{£281,000k} \times 100$	$\dfrac{£41,500k}{£596,000k} \times 100$
	= 10.50%	= 6.96%
Capital turnover		
$\dfrac{\text{Revenue}}{\text{Capital employed}}$	$\dfrac{£354,900k}{£281,000k}$	$\dfrac{£706,260k}{£596,000k}$
	= 1.26 times	= 1.19 times
Gross profit margin		
$\dfrac{\text{Gross profit}}{\text{Revenue}} \times 100$	$\dfrac{£71,400k}{£354,900k} \times 100$	$\dfrac{£156,200k}{£706,260k} \times 100$
	= 20.12%	= 22.12%
Operating profit margin		
$\dfrac{\text{Operating profit}}{\text{Revenue}} \times 100$	$\dfrac{£29,500k}{£354,900K} \times 100$	$\dfrac{£41,500k}{£706,260k} \times 100$
	= 8.31%	= 5.88%

(b) Interpretation

Marsh Ltd has a better return on capital employed because the company generated proportionally higher profits from less capital employed, while Mallow Ltd generated proportionally lower profits from a larger amount of capital employed. The capital turnover ratio helps explain the reasons: Marsh Ltd turned over the capital employed in the company to generate revenue just over 1¼ times during the year, whereas capital employed was used slight less frequently during the year in Mallow Ltd. The superior gross profit margin for Mallow Ltd suggests that the company has a lower cost of sales than Marsh Ltd. However, the superior operating profit margin for Marsh Ltd suggests the company is controlling its operating costs better than Mallow Ltd.

3. Ted Baker 2012 and 2011

The brief notes below each pair of ratios give guidance on the purpose of the ratio and the key points to be covered when interpreting the ratios.

(i) Dividend per share

	2012	2011
$\dfrac{\text{Total dividends}}{\text{No. ordinary shares}}$ [× 100 for pence]	$\dfrac{9{,}744k}{43{,}209k} \times 100$	$\dfrac{8{,}574k}{41{,}786k} \times 100$
	= 22.55 pence	= 20.52 pence

Investment ratio that measures the amount of dividend on one ordinary share.

Good news for investors: Up by just over 2p, despite slight increase in number of shares.

Some profits retained.

(ii) Dividend yield

	2012	2011
$\dfrac{\text{Dividend per share}}{\text{Average share price}} \times 100$	$\dfrac{22.55p}{478.00p} \times 100$	$\dfrac{20.52p}{441.40p} \times 100$
	= 4.72%	= 4.65%

Investment ratio that measures the dividend per share in relation to the average price of the share.

Good news: Increase reflects higher dividend per share and increased average share price.

(iii) Earnings per share (EPS)

	2012	2011
$\dfrac{\text{Profit for ordinary shareholders}}{\text{No. of ordinary shares}}$ [× 100 for pence]	$\dfrac{£17{,}557k}{43{,}209k} \times 100$	$\dfrac{£17{,}280k}{41{,}786} \times 100$
	= 40.63 pence	= 41.35 pence

Investment ratio that measures the amount of profit earned by one ordinary share.

Reflects the total profit (including retained profit) attributable to ordinary shareholders.

No significant change: Slightly lower profit relative to number of shares. Contrast with dividend per share.

(iv) Price/earnings (P/E)

	2012	2011
Average share price	478.00p	441.40p
Earnings per share	40.63p	41.35p
	= 11.76 years	= 10.67 years

Investment ratio that compares the amount invested in one share with EPS and reflects the stock market's confidence in how long the current level of EPS will be sustained.

Good news for investors: Number of years the market believes company has good prospects has increased by just over 1 year – reflects growing optimism in the stock market.

(v) Return on equity (ROE)

	2012	2011
$\dfrac{\text{Profit for ordinary shareholders}}{\text{Equity}} \times 100$	$\dfrac{£17,557k}{£85,185k} \times 100$	$\dfrac{£17,280k}{£76,024k} \times 100$
	= 20.61%	= 22.73%

A profitability ratio that measures return on shareholders' funds.

No significant change: Now lower at £20.61 for every £100 equity, but better than risk free interest rate.

(vi) Return on capital employed (ROCE)

	2012	2011
$\dfrac{\text{Operating profit}}{\text{CE (Equity + Non-current liabilities)}} \times 100$	$\dfrac{£24,269k}{£86,605k} \times 100$	$\dfrac{£24,132k}{£77,571k} \times 100$
	= 28.02%	= 31.11%

Profitability ratio that measures the percentage return on total funds (equity + long-term debt) and the ability of management to generate revenue and control costs (stewardship).

Unlike return on equity, it includes debt finance.

Bad news: Now only £28.02 operating profit for every £100 of capital employed despite increased capital.

Better than risk free interest rate.

ROE is lower than ROCE as it takes account of finance costs by using profit after interest and tax.

(vii) Operating profit margin

	2012	2011
$\dfrac{\text{Operating profit}}{\text{Revenue}} \times 100$	$\dfrac{£24,269k}{£215,625k} \times 100$	$\dfrac{£24,132k}{£187,700k} \times 100$
	$= 11.26\%$	$= 12.86\%$

Profitability ratio that measures the percentage return per £1 of revenue based on operating profit.

Bad news: Now only £11.26 operating profit per £100 revenue. Suggests lower selling prices and/or rising operating costs.

(viii) Capital turnover

	2012	2011
$\dfrac{\text{Revenue}}{\text{CE (Equity + Non-current liabilities)}}$	$\dfrac{£215,625k}{£86,605k}$	$\dfrac{£187,700k}{£77,571k}$
	$= 2.49$ times	$= 2.42$ times

Profitability ratio that measures the number of times capital employed was used to achieve revenue.

No significant change in the efficient use of capital invested. Need to compare with competitors.

Important guide to pricing and purchasing policies in retail sector.

4. Ted Baker 2012 and 2011 (continued)

The brief notes below each pair of ratios shown below give guidance on the purpose of the ratio and the key points to be covered when interpreting the ratios.

(i) Current ratio

	2012	2011
$\dfrac{\text{Current assets}}{\text{Current liabilities}}$	$\dfrac{£91,837k}{£46,487k}$	$\dfrac{£83,800k}{£39,186k}$
	$= 1.98:1$	$= 2.14:1$

Liquidity ratio that measures the relationship between current assets and short-term liabilities.

Lower but no cause for concern: Now £1.98 current assets for every £1 current liability. But current assets include inventory which cannot be converted into cash at short notice.

(ii) Acid test

	2012	2011
Current assets − Inventory	£39,965k	£41,308k
Current liabilities	£46,487k	£39,186k
	= 0.86:1	= 1.05:1

Liquidity ratio that measures the relationship between liquid assets and short-term liabilities.

Lower but no cause for concern: Now £0.86 liquid assets for every £1 current liability, but accounts are prudence based and it is good financial management to obtain longer credit period with suppliers than given to customers.

Assures lenders that the business is a going concern.

(iii) Inventory holding period (months)

	2012	2011
$\dfrac{\text{Closing inventory}}{\text{Cost of sales}} \times 12$	$\dfrac{£51,872k}{£83,419k} \times 12$	$\dfrac{£42,492k}{£71,923k} \times 12$
	= 7.46 months	= 7.09 months

Efficiency ratio that measures average time between purchase and sale of inventory.

No significant change: Management has moved inventory slightly less quickly this year, so possibility of higher storage costs. Slightly longer than one fashion season, but no major cause for concern.

(iv) Trade receivables collection period (months)

	2012	2011
$\dfrac{\text{Trade receivables}}{\text{Revenue}} \times 12$	$\dfrac{£19,744k}{£215,625} \times 12$	$\dfrac{£18,182k}{£187,700k} \times 12$
	= 1.10 months	= 1.16 months

Efficiency ratio that measures the average time customers took to settle their debts.

Stable: In both years the average period was about 1 month.

Suggests efficient credit control.

(v) Trade payables payment period (months)

	2012	2011
$\dfrac{\text{Trade payables}}{\text{Cost of sales}} \times 12$	$\dfrac{£15,910k}{£83,419k} \times 12$	$\dfrac{£18,888k}{£71,923k} \times 12$
	= 2.29 months	= 3.15 months

Efficiency ratio that measures the average time taken to pay suppliers.

Average period has decreased by nearly 1 month, suggesting suppliers have reduced the credit period.

(vi) Debt/equity

	2012	2011
$\dfrac{\text{Non-current liabilities}}{\text{Equity}} \times 100$	$\dfrac{£1,420k}{£85,185k} \times 100$	$\dfrac{£1,547k}{£76,024k} \times 100$
	= 1.67%	= 2.03%

Gearing ratio that describes financial structure/relationship between long-term debt and shareholders' funds.

Good news: Still very low gearing (£1.67 long-term debt for £100 equity). Low risk to lenders.

(vii) Interest cover

	2012	2011
$\dfrac{\text{Operating profit}}{\text{Interest payable}}$	$\dfrac{£24,269k}{£208k}$	$\dfrac{£24,132k}{£65k}$
	= 116.68 times	= 371.26 times

Gearing ratio that measures the relative safety of interest payments.

Decrease but no cause for concern as interest payable can still be covered >100 times.

Low risk to long-term lenders that Ted Baker will be unable to pay interest.

5. Write an essay that discusses the strengths and weaknesses of ratio analysis as a technique for helping users such as investors, lenders and creditors make decisions about providing resources to a business.

Ratio analysis is 'the use of accounting ratios to evaluate a company's operating performance and financial stability… In conducting an analysis comparisons will be made with other companies and with industry averages over a period of time. The analysis of ratios can indicate how well a company is run, the risks of financial insolvency, and the financial returns provided' (Law, 2010, p. 345). The advantage of ratio analysis is that any number of ratios can be calculated to meet the needs of the user. The results of the analysis provide additional information that helps investors, lenders, creditors and other users of the financial statements make their different economic decisions.

Ratio analysis suffers from a number of general limitations. Apart from earnings per share (EPS), there are no agreed definitions of the terms used, so ratios based on different definitions will not be comparable. In addition, the figures needed to calculate the ratios may not be disclosed and less precise alternatives may have to be used. Comparative data is essential, but comparison is not possible for a new business. Comparative data may not be available for competitors (for example, industry benchmarks may not be available or the business may occupy a niche market). Care must be taken when comparing ratios with those of competitors as they may have adopted different accounting policies (for example, in respect of depreciation of PPE or valuation of inventory). Finally, it is important to note that figures in financial statements can be misleading if there is high inflation or unscrupulous manipulation.

Ratio analysis is also constrained by the general limitations of financial statements from which the figures are drawn. Financial statements only contain quantitative data. Therefore, ratio analysis does not take account of non-financial factors such as whether the business has sound plans for the future, a good reputation, a strong customer base, reliable suppliers, loyal employees, obsolete assets, strong competitors, poor industrial relations or activities in a high risk industry. Financial statements do not focus on any non-financial effects of transactions or events or reflect future transactions or events that may enhance or impair the entity's operations. In addition, they do not anticipate the impact of potential changes in the economic environment. A final point is that there is a substantial degree of classification and aggregation in the financial statements and the effect of allocating continuous operations to the reporting period (ASB, 1999).

Despite these drawbacks, ratio analysis is an invaluable tool that gives users an indication of where further investigation is required to gain better understanding of the present and future financial performance and stability of the business.

INDEX

A

abbreviated accounts, 47
accountability, 44
accountancy profession, 1–4
    code of ethics, 2
    membership of UK and
        Irish accountancy
        bodies, 2
accounting, 4, 5
    definition, 4
    purpose, 5
    system, 15, 17
Accounting Directives, 46
accounting equation, 18, 85
accounting principles, 6,
        39–43
    accruals concept, 41
    business entity
        concept, 42
    consistency concept, 42
    definition, 39
    going concern
        assumption, 40
    historical cost concept, 42
    matching concept, 41
    materiality concept, 42
    money measurement
        concept, 42
    period concepts, 41
    prudence concept, 42
    realisation concept, 41
accounting standards, 45,
        48–50
    definition, 48
    EU-adopted IFRS, 49
    FRS, 49
    IAS and IFRS, 49
accounts preparation, 6

accrual accounting, 41, 62,
        108
accruals (accrued
        expenses), 70, 92
accruals concept, 41
acid test, 165, 166
administrative expenses, 62,
        75, 93
advisory services, 7
Alternative Investment
        Market (AIM), 46
annual report and
        accounts, 43, 149
assets
    definition, 18
    recording in the
        accounts, 20
Association of Chartered
        Certified Accountants
        (ACCA), 2
Association of International
        Accountants, 2
audit, definition, 45
audit exemption, 47
auditing, 1, 6, 45
auditors' report, 43, 45, 47

B

bad debts, 74, 95
    definition, 74
balancing the accounts, 31
big GAAP, 47
bookkeeping, 6, 17–19
business combination, 130
    definition, 131
business entities, 7–13
business entity concept, 42
Business Names Act 1985, 10

C

capital
    definition, see equity
    recording in the
        accounts, 20
    share capital, 86
capital expenditure, 87
capital turnover, 163
carriage inward and
        outward, 34
cash, 110–11
    definition, 111
cash deficit and
        surplus, 109
cash equivalents, 110–11
    definition, 111
cash flows, 111–23
cash inflows and outflows,
        definition, 109
    from financing
        activities, 112
    from investing
        activities, 111
    from operating
        activities, 111, 113, 117
    see also statement of cash
        flows
Chartered Accountants
        Ireland (CAI), 2
Chartered Institute
        of Management
        Accountants (CIMA), 2
Chartered Institute of
        Public Finance and
        Accountancy (CIPFA), 2
Code of Ethics for
        Professional
        Accountants, 2, 3

Companies Act 2006
(CA2006), 11, 12, 46
Companies Act (Strategic
Report and Directors'
Reports) Regulations
2013, 44
company, 7, 11, 12
company law, 45, 46–7, 50
comparability, 54
comprehensive income, 53,
57, 58, 61
Conceptual Framework
for Financial
Reporting, 50–4
definition, 51
consistency concept, 42, 54
consolidated financial
statements, 130–49
consolidated statement of
changes in equity, 131,
148
consolidated statement of
comprehensive
income, 131, 145–6
consolidated statement of
financial position, 131
at acquisition, 135
after acquisition, 142–3
control of an investee, 132–4
definition, 132
convergence and
harmonisation of
financial
reporting, 49, 50
corporate governance, 49
corporate recovery, 7
corporate social
responsibility, 44
cost of sales, 63, 67
credit entries in the
accounts, 19
credit risk, 51
credit transactions, 28
current cost, 42, 59
current ratio, 165

D
debit entries in the
accounts, 19
debt/equity ratio, 170
depreciable amount, 72, 93
definition, 72
depreciation, 71–3, 93–5
definition, 72
diminishing balance
method, 94
straight-line method, 73
discounts allowed and
received, 35
distribution costs, 63, 75
dividend per share, 157
dividend yield, 158
double-entry
bookkeeping, 17–19
definition, 18
doubtful receivables
allowance, 74, 95
definition, 74

E
earnings per share, 159
economic transactions,
definition, 4
efficiency ratios, 165–8
inventory holding
period, 167
trade payables payment
period, 168
trade receivables collection
period, 168
elements of financial
statements, 56–60
recognition and
measurement, 58–60
elements of UK
GAAP, 45
enhancing qualitative
characteristics of
usefulness, 54
environmental and social
reporting, 44

equity, 18, 57, 84, 86
definition, 18
ethics and the professional
accountant, 2
EU Accounting Directives, 46
expenses, 57, 59, 61
administrative
expenses, 63, 75
definition, 23
recording in the
accounts, 22

F
fair value, 42, 59, 72, 73
definition, 135
faithful representation, 53
finance costs, 64
financial accounting
definition, 6
purpose, 5
financial performance, 57, 61
financial position, 57, 84
financial reporting, 39, 43–4,
47, 50
definition, 44
harmonisation and
convergence, 49, 50
objective of general
purpose reporting, 51
regulatory
framework, 43–6
Financial Reporting Council
(FRC), 49
Financial Reporting Standard
for Smaller Entities
(FRSSE), 50
financial reporting standards
(FRSs), see individual
standards
financial statement
analysis, 152
limitations, 173
trend analysis, 171–2
financial statements, 56–60
elements of, 56, 57, 58

financing activities,
definition, 112
FRS 100, *Application of Financial Reporting Requirements*, 49
FRS 101, *Reduced Disclosure Framework*, 49
FRS 102, *The Financial Reporting Standard Applicable in the UK and Republic of Ireland*, 49
FRS 105, *The Financial Reporting Standard applicable to the Micro-Entities Regime*, 49–50
fundamental accounting principles, 39–43
fundamental qualitative characteristics of usefulness, 53

G
GAAP, *see* Generally Accepted Accounting Practice
gearing ratios, 153, 169–70
debt/equity ratio, 170
interest cover, 170
general purpose financial reporting, 51
Generally Accepted Accounting Practice (GAAP), 45
going concern assumption, 40
goodwill, 71, 117, 137
definition, 135
impairment of, 117, 143
gross profit, 63
definition, 64
gross profit margin, 164
group accounts, *see* consolidated financial statements

H
harmonisation and convergence of financial reporting, 49, 50
historical cost concept, 42

I
IAS 1, *Presentation of Financial Statements*, 56, 64, 85, 131
IAS 2, *Inventories*, 69, 92
IAS 16, *Property, Plant and Equipment*, 71, 93
IAS 36, *Impairment of Assets*, 143
IFRS 3, *Business Combinations*, 130, 135
IFRS 10, *Consolidated Financial Statements*, 131, 132
IFRS for SMEs, 49, 64, 68, 69, 71, 72, 85, 92, 93
IFRS Foundation, 49
income, 22, 57, 61
definition, 23
other income (non-sales revenue), 35, 63
recognition and measurement, 58
initial public offering (IPO), 184
Institute of Chartered Accountants in England and Wales (ICAEW), 2
Institute of Chartered Accountants in Scotland (ICAS), 2
interest cover, 229
International Accounting Standards Board (IASB), 49, 50

International Ethics Standards Board for Accountants (IESBA), 2
International Federation of Accountants (IFAC), 2
International Financial Reporting Standards (IFRSs), 49
inventory, 15, 69, 92
opening and closing inventory, 34
recording in the accounts, 25
inventory holding period, 167
investing activities, 111–12
definition 112
investment ratios, 153, 157
dividend per share, 157
dividend yield, 158
earnings per share, 159
price-earnings ratio, 160
investment risk, 51

J
joint and several liability, 9
joint control, 220

L
ledger, 19
lending risk, 51
liabilities
current, 86
definition, 18
non-current, 86
recording in the accounts, 20
limitations
of ratio analysis, 173–4
of trial balance, 77
limited company, 11
limited liability
definition, 12
limited liability partnership (LLP), 9
liquidation, 40

liquidity, 57, 88, 109
liquidity ratios, 153, 165
    acid test, 165
    current ratio, 165
little GAAP, 47
loans, 12, 40, 51
    loan account, 20
London Stock Exchange, 12

M

management accounting,
    purpose, 6
matching concept, 41
materiality concept, 42
micro-entities, 47, 50
money measurement
    concept, 42

N

net cash flow,
    definition, 109
net realisable value, 42,
    69, 92
non-controlling interest
    (NCI), definition, 134
non-sales revenue, 35, 63

O

operating activities, 111
    cash flows from, 111, 113,
    117
    definition, 112
operating profit, 63–4
    definition, 64
operating profit margin, 164
    trend, 171–2
other income, 35, 63
other reserves, 86

P

parent entity, 130, 132
Partnership Act 1890, 10
partnerships, 7, 9
period concept, 41
petty cash, 35

post trial balance
    adjustments, 68, 91
power of an investor,
    definition, 132
prepayments (prepaid
    expenses), 69, 70, 92
    definition, 70
price-earnings ratio, 160
private company, 12
profit for the period, 67
profitability ratios, 153, 161–5
    capital turnover, 163
    gross profit margin, 164
    operating profit
        margin, 164
    return on capital
        employed, 161
    return on equity, 161
property, plant and
    equipment, 71–3, 85
    definition, 71
    depreciation, 71–3, 93–5
prudence concept, 42
public company, 12
purchases, 26
purchases returns, 27

Q

qualitative characteristics of
    usefulness, 53

R

ratio analysis, 152–3, 157–74
    efficiency ratios, 165–8
    gearing ratios, 153,
        169–71
    investment ratios, 153,
        157–60
    limitations, 173
    liquidity ratios, 153, 165
    profitability ratios, 153,
        161–5
    trend analysis, 171–2
realisable value, 42, 69, 92
realisation concept, 41

regulatory framework
    for financial
    reporting, 43–6
relevance, 53
residual value, 71
    definition, 72
retained earnings, 86
return on capital employed, 161
return on equity, 161
returns inward and
    outward, 27
revenue
    definition, 23
    recording in the accounts, 22
revenue expenditure, 87

S

sales, 26
sales returns, 27
share capital, 86
shareholder, 11
small and medium-sized
    entities (SMEs), 8
sole proprietorship, 7, 9
source documents, 15–17
stakeholders, 40, 58
statement of cash
    flows, 108–25
statement of changes in
    equity, 57, 148
statement of comprehensive
    income, 56, 61–79
statement of financial
    position, 58, 84–103
stewardship, definition, 45
stock exchange rules, 45
stocktaking, 65

T

timeliness, 54
trade credit, 12
trade payables, 28
    trade payables payment
        period, 168

trade receivables, 28
  trade receivables collection
    period, 168
trend analysis, 171–2
trial balance, 31–6
  definition, 33
  limitations, 35–6
true and fair view,
    6, 45

U
UK GAAP, 45
underlying assumptions
  accrual accounting, 41
  going concern, 40
understandability, 54
unlimited liability, 9
useful life, 71–2
  definition, 72

users of general purpose
    financial statements, 51, 52

V
verifiability, 54
voting rights of investors, 132

W
working capital, 165